Other Titles in this Series

John Abbott

IMPROVISATION IN REHEARSAL

Foreword by Mark Rylance

NICK HERN BOOKS
London
www.nickhernbooks.co.uk

A NICK HERN BOOK

Improvisation in Rehearsal
first published in Great Britain in 2009
by Nick Hern Books Limited
14 Larden Road, London W3 7ST

Cover designed by Peter Bennett
Typeset by Nick Hern Books
Printed and bound in Great Britain
by Athenaeum Press Ltd, Gateshead, Tyne and Wear

A CIP catalogue record for this book is available
from the British Library

ISBN 978 1 85459 523 2

This book is printed on FSC-accredited paper
made from trees from sustainable forests.

Contents

For Jane

Foreword
by Mark Rylance

WHEN I TRAINED TO BE AN ACTOR IN THE LATE SEVENTIES my favourite class took place on Friday afternoon with Ben Benison of Theatre Machine: improvisation. It was always unexpected and magical, and I learnt the crucial lesson, applicable to all other disciplines, and still essential to every moment on the stage: whatever the other actor offers you, you first say 'yes'. 'Yes', even if your answer is 'no'.

You must receive what is given. Harder than you would think; many actors fake it. I have caught myself faking it without knowing it. Actually, it is all you have to do. Certainly all you have to prepare to do backstage and the cure for all stage disease, rot and stagnation.

I had arrived from the Midwest of America, aged eighteen, my head in the clouds of fears and fantasy about the precise technique of English acting. I thought everything should be sealed and delivered to an audience and to your fellow actors, precise, repeated, controlled, planned. Improvisation was for amateurs and besides, it was terrifying and extremely vulnerable.

To my great surprise, the best teachers at RADA were interested in life! Spontaneous, unplanned, imprecise, uncontrolled, unrepeatable life! And the place that this happened most of all was when we improvised. Yes, it was still terrifying and vulnerable. I fell in love with it.

I believe all rehearsals, all playing, benefits from a spirit of improvisation. Spontaneous life is what I want to hear and see when I witness acting. I want to experience people who are really lost, confused and vulnerable. Trust is required and improvisation builds this trust and presence.

I think I first met John Abbott above a betting shop in Brixton where I was planning to raise a storm in a stone circle and needed a king to climb through a maze of yellow school desks in search of his lost son. Something like that. John was the king of that Stone Circle Tempest, generous, joyous, patient, committed on all levels. I can still see him looking out over yellow fields of rape, castle embankments, and the concrete foundations of Sam Wanamaker's Globe Theatre Project, searching for his drowned child.

Later we celebrated his fiftieth birthday reading and discussing *Moby Dick* over many weeks. That work never grew into the production we had imagined. Our lives took us onto distant oceans, pursuing our individual white whales.

John helped me to create the sonnet walks between Westminster Abbey and the Globe Theatre, inspiring audiences and actors with his wonderful street-theatre creations. Recently we spent a lovely St George's Day watching his students follow in his footsteps along the Thames.

I'm not surprised that John has found such joy teaching young actors. He delights in theatre and I'm sure this, his second book on improvisation, will inspire and delight its readers into a spontaneous 'Yes!'

Author's Note

I STARTED OUT AS AN OBSESSIVE AND ENTHUSIASTIC AMATEUR (The Sunbury Sofisticats); trained at the Central School of Speech and Drama (George Hall, Cicely Berry, Litz Pisk); plunged into the dying days of repertory theatre (Agatha Christie, *Salad Days*); caught the tail-end of black-and-white television (*Z Cars, Softly Softly*); got involved in the birth of the London fringe (The Half Moon, The Gate); became a member of the Royal Shakespeare Company (*Richard II, The Taming of the Shrew*); settled into a comfortable career of TV (*Dr Who, Emmerdale Farm, Trial and Retribution*); made a few films (*Four Weddings and a Funeral, The Young Poisoner's Handbook*) and commercials (too numerous to mention); made enough money to buy a house and raise two kids – and eventually I got a proper job as an acting teacher.

My knowledge of rehearsal techniques has been influenced by the many directors I worked with. My thanks go out to the following:

Malcolm Everett, who introduced me to the joy of putting on a show (The Sunbury Sofisticats).

Peter Oyston, who showed me how to explore the depths of a character (Central School of Speech and Drama).

Guy Sprung, who was the first person to ask me to improvise a scene (The original Half Moon Theatre in Allie Street).

Christopher Sandford, who asked me and a group of actors to create a whole play through improvisation (T.I.E. at The Duke's Playhouse, Lancaster).

Simon Oates, who gave me the best instruction ever on how to play a love scene: 'For f**k's sake, John, stop acting. Just stand there, look at her and say the lines' (Everyman Theatre, Cheltenham).

John Barton, who proved that academia and theatrical flare are brilliant bedfellows (The Royal Shakespeare Company, Stratford-upon-Avon).

Andrew Dallmeyer, who tore the third wall to shreds and taught me how to genuinely mystify an audience (The Elusive Theatre Company, anywhere and everywhere).

Lou Stein, who made his actors behave as if a grubby room above a pub was the National Theatre (The Gate Theatre, Notting Hill).

Jonathan Moore, who introduced me to anarchy in the theatre (The New London Actors).

Mike Alfreds, who proved that life on stage is more important than a perfectly honed machine (The Cambridge Arts Theatre).

Mark Rylance, who is the master of research, experimentation, originality and truth (Phoebus Cart Theatre Company).

And Jane Harrison, who showed me that teaching all this is a massively rewarding occupation for an older man (The School of Acting, ArtsEd).

I want to thank Nick Hern, for his confidence in me and I also want to thank all his dedicated and charming staff. Most importantly thanks to Matt Applewhite, who has yet again helped me to get a book into shape and onto the shelves.

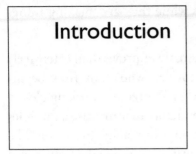

Introduction

FOR MOST PEOPLE, THE ONLY THING THEY KNOW ABOUT improvisation is the sort of madcap humour that was featured on the hit TV show *Whose Line is it Anyway?* People in the audience shouted out random ideas to a bunch of highly skilled stand-up comedians who were then brilliant at making things up on the spot. They had crazy conversations, threw their bodies around and behaved like clowns or robots or animals or whatever they thought would be funny. Their reactions were lightning-fast and they had incredibly inventive minds, but as far as improvisation was concerned, their main preoccupation was getting laughs. Entertaining the audience.

But improvisation can be many other things. Musicians improvise. Storytellers improvise. Dancers improvise. Chefs, teachers and salesmen improvise. And, of course, actors improvise.

Actors can be just as creative as the comedians on *Whose Line is it Anyway?*, but rather than making people laugh, they can improvise with true emotions and an honest belief in their spontaneous creations in order to explore all the genres of text-based drama. Sometimes their improvisations may be funny because real-life situations can be funny, but they can also be tragic, mysterious, romantic, thrilling, poignant or scary. Human beings experience so many different emotions and moods, and if the actors find the truth of an improvisation they can explore all these emotions while they are 'making things up on the spot'.

Mike Leigh uses this sort of dramatic improvisation extensively when he asks his actors to improvise a whole film from beginning to end. Even more conventional directors working closely to a script will sometimes get the actors to improvise a few lines in order to bring the natural rhythms of real life to a scene. The results can be dynamic and surprising, but like the improvised scenes on *Whose Line is it Anyway?* these improvisations are made to be watched. They are part of the entertainment.

But improvisation can also be used as part of the creative process of rehearsing a play. It can be a fabulous tool for exploration and discovery. It can strengthen the actor's commitment to their character. And it can create an environment of confidence and spontaneity.

This book sets out to explore the many ways in which improvisation can be used during the rehearsal process of plays or musicals. Many of the techniques described can also be used as part of the preparation for filming, but I have focused on stage productions because that is my area of expertise. The improvisations can be used with both amateur and professional actors, on school plays and devised pieces, and they can be used on scripts both old and new.

Directors who have never used improvisation in rehearsal will, I hope, find lots of useful suggestions in this book. Even directors who are old-hands at using improvisation techniques should find some new and interesting ideas. I have outlined various improvisation possibilities for each stage of the rehearsal process, from the actor's first stumbling steps to the final refinements of the whole play, so there should be fresh ideas for introducing improvisation into the mix throughout the entire rehearsal period.

Although this book is primarily for directors, it can also be used by actors who may want to include improvisation as part of their personal preparation. The chapters that deal with character creation can be particularly useful since they deal with solo improvisations. Also, several like-minded actors working on a production may want to try some of the relationship improvisations while the director is rehearsing other scenes. Of course, it is always preferable for the actors to tell the director about the improvisations they intend to work on, but most directors are pleased to have the cast put in the extra work and they may even be inspired to set up some improvisations of their own.

Finally, of course, I hope this book will be useful to drama teachers. They are the ones that are introducing the dramatic form to a new generation. They are awakening the creative spirit in young people and they are nurturing tomorrow's talent. They have a tremendous responsibility and I hope this book will give them plenty of ideas and support.

Rehearsals

A group of people get together with a script. Words on paper. Mostly dialogue. Several weeks later they present a realistic, fleshed-out, three-dimensional version of a story by standing up in front of an audience and speaking the dialogue of the script. What happens in between? How do they make those 'words on paper' come alive? What do they do in rehearsals?

There are many answers to these questions because actors and directors use many different rehearsal techniques to help them achieve their ends. Probably the most famous acting teacher in the world was the Russian director Konstantin Stanislavsky who created and ran the Moscow Art Theatre over a hundred years ago. Apart from being a champion of the budding playwright Anton Chekhov and directing most of his plays, Stanislavsky wrote several books about the rehearsal process, analysing and refining techniques to enable actors to present truthful versions of their characters. Some of his rehearsal techniques have been isolated and developed by other people. Some have been exploited and heavily elaborated. Stanislavsky himself was always one for trying out new methods but towards the end of his working life, it seems pretty clear that he felt that the most useful technique for actors to use during the rehearsal process was improvisation.

As a rehearsal technique, improvisation exploits the actor's imagination. It allows them to experience certain events, emotions and relationships in order to find a truthful way of thinking and behaving as their character. It's a way of exploring, experimenting and making discoveries through actual experience.

The Actor's Fear

Acting seems to be such an easy thing to do. As Noël Coward said: 'Speak clearly, don't bump into the furniture and if you must have motivation, think of your pay packet on Friday.' So if you are the sort of person that is not afraid of doing things in front of other people, then acting would seem to be a doddle. Wouldn't it?

Actually, it's pretty hard when you consider all the qualities and skills that actors require. They must have a good understanding of human psychology. They have to transform themselves physically. They often have to expose their own inner emotions in front of other people. They need to possess an intelligent understanding of the writer's intentions, and a working knowledge of the way people use language. They should know quite a lot of history and have an understanding of historical social conventions. They also have to perform all manner of tasks as if they were natural to them. (I once watched Donald Sinden cook a whole meal during the course of a play because his character was a celebrity chef.) But perhaps the hardest thing actors have to do is to work intimately and productively with other creative people. People who may have very different ideas about the play, the characters and the emotions of a scene. Think that's easy? It's not. It's nerve-wracking.

As an actor I was often nervous in rehearsals because I was frightened of 'getting things wrong', but I always felt more confident when I 'became' my character and submerged myself into his imaginary world. Let's face it, despite all the necessary skills I have itemised in the last paragraph, the most important tool in the actor's creative toolkit is an uninhibited imagination.

The Actor's Imagination

Actors often seem to be rather childish. I mean, what sort of job is that for a grown-up? Pretending to be other people. That's what kids do. But we all love to watch stories being acted out so we *need* actors because they are the ones who can do the job. They are the ones who are able to tap into a 'let's pretend' state of mind. That's not easy for other people but that's exactly what actors do. They allow part of their brain to believe that they are actually someone else in the same way that children can believe they are astronauts or television presenters. When actors are at work, they can make themselves feel like they are detectives or lovers or doctors or whatever the part requires, and that helps the rest of us believe in the story.

Actors also try to believe in the reality of any particular moment. If another character points a stage gun at an actor during a scene, the actor imagines that the gun is real and that the other character is a dangerous, psychopathic killer, and by doing that, the actor actually starts to feel frightened. That makes his or her reaction more truthful, conveying a genuine emotion to the audience who consequently better understand the character's fear.

This ability to feel and convey the truth of an imaginary situation is a highly prized skill that actors have. They love to use it. It solves loads of their problems. Ask a non-actor how they would behave if someone pointed a gun at them and they would think about all the different reactions they might have and come up with some sort of answer. 'I'd probably run away.' Ask the same question of an actor and he or she would say, 'Pretend you are pointing a gun at me and I'll let you know.' They are able to tap into the truth of a situation and by doing that they discover the appropriate emotional response.

Improvisation can exploit this fantastic ability to pretend in order to answer questions, develop complex characters and relationships, and solve all sorts of problems during the rehearsal of a play.

Naturalistic Improvisation

When improvisation is used in rehearsals, the actors should believe in their characters and find the truth of the improvised situation as much as they can. They should never try to entertain other people in the rehearsal room because that will destroy the fragile web of reality that they are trying to create. If a part of the actor's mind is thinking about the effect their improvisation will have on the people who are watching, then they won't be concentrating on the truth. In fact, improvisation in rehearsal can work just as well if no one, not even the director, is watching because the sole purpose is to allow the actors to experience various situations as if they were actually happening and to learn from their own reactions.

The Director's Role

When actors are improvising it's important for the director to keep a low profile. A critical eye can make the actor lose sight of reality either through panic or the desire to perform, particularly if they are struggling with a character. A relaxed struggle is often more productive than a struggle made tense through observation and criticism. I usually try to watch rehearsal improvisations unnoticed, by standing to one side, or lurking in the shadows. If they are given the time and the opportunity, actors will often sort problems out for themselves during an improvisation. And these solutions are often more deeply embedded in reality than when the actor is desperately trying to fulfil a partially understood concept given to them by the director. Let the actors do their work, I say. Trust them. They can work it out.

The Director's Feedback

Of course, the director's observations are always useful for the actor, but directors should never criticise an actor's work after an improvisation because that can inhibit the creative spirit. It doesn't matter whether the improvisations were good or bad, what matters is what the actors have learned during the experience. Improvisation is a risky business with many pitfalls because the actors are flying without a safety net, so a sympathetic critique from the director will be much more valuable than negative criticism. In the discussions after an improvisation I often try to 'nudge' the actor in the direction I think he or she ought to go, rather than picking out what was wrong. If I focus on the positives, the negatives will generally disappear.

An Open Mind

Before starting an improvisation the actors should 'become' their characters as much as they can. They can't know everything about the character because the whole purpose of this work is to find things out, but they can concentrate on what they have discovered so far. They must also know what their character wants from the improvised scene – their character's objective – and they must be responsive to the other actors' creativity by listening and reacting. Sometimes an improvisation will take the actors down unexpected paths and they will have to abandon some of their preconceived ideas. This is great. In order to use improvisation as part of the creative process, the actors must learn to cast aside preconceptions and keep an open mind.

That's all there is to it. The actors should believe in the truth of the improvisation and go with the flow. They should never feel obliged to speak if their character doesn't feel like it and they should never do anything their character doesn't want to do. The actors should just be truthful to their instincts, be 'in the moment' and above all (I can't overstate this): *they should never try to entertain.*

Discoveries

When you're travelling through unexplored territory, you can sometimes take the wrong path and arrive at a useless dead-end. The same thing can happen when improvisation is used as a method of exploration. Any journey into the unknown will produce unexpected results and some of these results can be totally unproductive. But on the other hand it's worth the trip because there is always the possibility of wonderful rewards. The path through the jungle that seems to be going nowhere can suddenly lead to a hidden Aztec city. Imagine what would happen if someone in the expedition had said, 'This path isn't working. Let's give up and turn back.' True, they wouldn't waste any exploration time, but on the other hand, there would be no possibility of Aztec gold.

It's the same with improvisations in rehearsal. If the results were known in advance there would be no point in doing the improvisation, and if you give up because the improvisation seems to be going nowhere, then there will be no possibility of amazing discoveries. When an improvisation seems to be going off-track, my advice is to persevere. Sometimes the actors will make the right adjustments and sometimes not, but whatever happens, there will be food for thought and plenty to talk about.

When improvisation is used early on in rehearsal there can also be a problem with facts. Although there may have been a thorough analysis of the text and a certain amount of research, it's still the beginning of a long journey and sometimes actors will make wrong assumptions about a character, or their imaginations will create impossible relationships which could never be supported by the text. When this happens during an improvisation it is still better to persevere because the actors may be in a very creative zone with free-flowing imaginations and it's best not to inhibit that creativity. Any incorrect facts or assumptions can become the focus of a discussion after the improvisation has finished. Stopping an improvisation because one of the actors has got a fact wrong would be like an explorer realising they are wearing the wrong boots and deciding to turn back just before they round the corner to the Aztec city. Don't worry about the mistakes. Battle on with sore feet. You never know what you might discover.

Exploration and Experimentation

I talk about exploration and experimentation a lot throughout this book because that is what rehearsals are for. To my mind, the whole of the rehearsal period should be about trying things out and not about polishing and refining half-formed discoveries. The explorations should be ongoing. There is no 'right way' of saying a line. There is no ultimate version of a character. There is no perfect production of a play. There is only the event that happens at the time that it's happening – and that's the performance. The performance is a work of art being created *at that moment* in front of the audience. So not only should every second of the rehearsal process be about new explorations and discoveries, but so should every second of every performance. If actors spend the rehearsal period trying to 'get things right' and 'practising to make perfect' then they are wasting valuable discovery time. If their performance is a perfectly honed version of something they discovered in the second week of rehearsal and they try to repeat it exactly the same way every night, then all they are doing is presenting the audience with a hollow reproduction and not a work of art. Go visit the Van Gogh Museum in Amsterdam and you will appreciate the difference. His paintings of sunflowers and fields of crows are far more vibrant and full of life than even the best reproductions in the most expensive art books.

Let's create works of art on stage, not 'perfect' copies.

—

Using This Book

This book is about using improvisation in the rehearsal of a play, but since all plays are different it's impossible to outline a series of improvisations that would be useful each and every time. So rather than giving a clear set of instructions, I've tried to identify various stages of the rehearsal process and then I've made suggestions and given examples of how improvisation can be used to help the actors build their characters, develop character relationships and solve rehearsal problems.

Each chapter starts with an anecdotal preamble which may or may not have something to do with the theatre. These stories and reflections always have an allegorical connection with the main thrust of the chapter and are there to stimulate the imagination. Actors are creative people and like to tell stories. After all, that is what their job is all about. As a director, I find that an allegory or a story can be a far more productive way to explain something to an actor than a simple description of what I want them to do. It gets their creative juices flowing and, before you know it, they have got the point. It helps them think for themselves and encourages a personal commitment to that new way of thinking.

Chapters 1 to 3 are about preparation and research. You can't just start using improvisation in rehearsals unless you have a good grounding of information. I feel it's important to outline my method for doing this, since some people may only be familiar with rehearsal processes that immediately start by acting out the dialogue. Actors often let their characters develop gradually as they rehearse a play with scripts in their hands, and research is slowly incorporated as the rehearsals proceed. But if you are going to ask actors to use improvisation in the early stages of rehearsal, they have to be properly prepared beforehand so their work is built on strong foundations. During these early chapters I describe both 'exercises' and 'improvisations'.

For the purposes of this book, an exercise – indicated with this symbol – is a rehearsal device which uses the actors' skills to develop an understanding of various aspects of the play, but doesn't necessarily require the actors to be in the role of their characters. As the director, I will often talk the actors through an exercise, feeding new ideas to them as they work.

On the other hand, an improvisation – signalled by this symbol – is when the actors 'become' their characters for a certain period of rehearsal time without any outside direction. This is usually done in pairs or in groups, but sometimes actors will be improvising on their own. To put it simply, whenever an actor is 'being' a character and trying to think and react in role for an extended period of time, without any external influence, then that is called an improvisation.

I tend to outline each particular exercise or improvisation and then give examples – generally as a separate boxed section containing this symbol. These describe how I have used improvisation in the rehearsal of a particular play. I hope this approach will give a good understanding of how the exercises and improvisations could be applied to other plays.

Chapters 4 to 7 describe how to use improvisation in the development of character and the exploration of relationships, and there are a number of exercises and improvisations that can be applied to most plays with a little adaptation.

The improvisations discussed in Chapters 8 to 11 are somewhat harder to describe since they are part of the creative process and would be different for every play. Generalised descriptions are almost impossible. In order to shed some light on my approach to using improvisation to solve rehearsal problems, I have described the rationale behind my choice of scenarios by giving specific examples. In doing this, I intend to reveal the possibilities of improvisation as a rehearsal technique and I hope that my examples will be a stimulus for your own creative thinking.

The Plays

Throughout this book I have made reference to specific plays in my discussion of improvisation techniques, and I often illustrate the work by referring to Frank McGuinness's play *Someone Who'll Watch Over Me*. It's a marvellous play about three people being held hostage in Lebanon and is well beyond the experience of most actors. As such, it is ripe for exploration through improvisation. Also, despite the fact that it only has three characters, the play embraces a web of shifting moods and relationships which need to be examined.

Where necessary I have tried to explain the plot, but it might be useful to read *Someone Who'll Watch Over Me* as a companion to this book. Anyway, I have no hesitation in recommending it. It's a very interesting play.

I also mention *A View from the Bridge* by Arthur Miller on several occasions. Like other American plays of the period, it contains some very complex and multifaceted relationships. I have attempted to outline any plot elements that you might need to know, but it would be better to read the play.

I also refer to several Shakespeare plays since they are likely to be known by most people, and they are full of fascinating plots, characters and relationships. A deeper knowledge of *Hamlet* would be useful since I mention it several times, but it's a great play and if you don't know it already, then you should read it.

Modern English should be used by the actors in all improvisations, even if you are rehearsing a play written or set in any other period of history. There is so much to think about that it would be asking far too much if the actors had to invent period dialogue or speak in verse while they were improvising a scene. A character is a character no matter what the sentence structure of the period. A relationship is a relationship whatever the vocabulary. And objectives, moods and social etiquette can be thoroughly explored without the use of heightened language.

I strongly believe that this experiential rehearsal process which uses improvisation extensively can be used on any play from any period because plays are about character, relationships and plot. I've used it on Shakespeare, William Wycherley, Oscar Wilde and Noël Coward. I've used it on Clifford Odets, Arthur Miller and Tennessee Williams. I've used it on Kaufman and Hart, Jim Cartwright and Harold Pinter. I've used it when I was directing a one-man show, although I had to use it selectively for obvious reasons, and I've seen it used on musicals and films. On every occasion it has added life and depth to the production, and so far I haven't experienced a rehearsal period where it wasn't massively helpful. Obviously, throughout this book I've referred to plays that are quite well-known, but improvisation can be used across the spectrum. The greenest first draft of a script can benefit from this technique just as much as a tried and tested classic.

Like Stanislavsky, I am a great believer in improvisation as a rehearsal tool and I use it a lot. Although each stage of the improvisation process described in this book can be used separately and in isolation, by using them all in the first part of the rehearsal period, I find that the actors are totally prepared when we start to rehearse the text of the play. The remainder of the rehearsal period is easier, more productive and great fun because each actor knows who their character is. They know how their character thinks and behaves, and they have a good understanding of their character's relationship with all the others in the play. If any problems occur later on in rehearsal, then an improvisation at any time will always shed new light on a scene.

There are loads of different ways that improvisation can be used in the creation of a play as a tool for exploration and discovery, and that is what this book is all about.

1

Preparation

I've never been skydiving but it must be tremendous fun. Swooping down from the clouds. Gliding through the sky like a golden eagle. Banking to the left. Diving to the right. Floating on an updraught with nothing holding you in place. Out there in empty space with the countryside like a perfect model village below. Little houses and roads. Trains moving through the hills like the most brilliant Hornby 'Double O' display at Harrods. Freedom. Flight. Harry Potter playing Quidditch. Leonardo's flying machine. The dream of mankind throughout the ages.

Mind you, skydiving wouldn't be such fun if you didn't know how to open your parachute. Can you imagine it? Or what if you fell out of a plane without wearing a parachute at all? That would detract somewhat from the fabulous flying experience. Or even if you had the parachute on, but you weren't sure if it was properly fitted. You'd be searching those little model buildings for a hospital so you could crash-land nearby. You'd be hoping to find a haystack in those glorious fields in order to guide yourself in the right direction. Yes, you would swoop and turn, but they would be the tactics of survival rather than the freedom of flight.

OK. Suppose you had your parachute on, and you had it properly fitted and you were reasonably sure it would open on time – what if you didn't know how to land? You might break your leg. Surely the landing anxiety would also detract from the magical skydiving experience. How could you glide like an eagle if you thought that pretty soon you wouldn't even be able to waddle like a duck?

No. Preparation is the thing. In order to skydive with the glorious dream of mankind making endorphins flow through your brain, you have to be fully prepared before you jump. You have to learn how to operate the parachute, and that includes packing it in the correct manner; fixing the harness safely; pulling the right cords to open it; guiding it in the direction you want to go; and landing without damaging your body. You also have to learn how to move around in free fall so you can go the way you want to. That's where the gliding, swooping and diving bit comes in. I've no idea how it's done, but I've seen it on television. It looks marvellous.

Once you have learned all the necessary skills you will be able to leap happily from an aeroplane and fly like a bird. Brilliant!

Preparation rules OK.

A CTORS ARE THE SORT OF PEOPLE WHO LIKE TO EXPRESS themselves by action. They like to *do* things. Directors structure things and give them clarity. I suppose you could say that they like to *illuminate* things. And writers use words to communicate ideas about the human condition. They *create* things. In the evolution of a play, it could be argued that writers use their intellect to create a text, directors use their imagination to visualise a production, and actors bring everything to life by expressing human emotions and actions with truth.

These breakdowns of different skills are generalisations, of course. Writers, directors and actors are all creative people;

they all like to illuminate things and all of them are people of action. We all have a bit of everything in us. But look at it this way: most people would agree that men are taller than women. However, in a group of twenty people, the tallest female would usually be taller than the shortest man. So forgive me for this oversimplification. What I'm talking about are *tendencies*. Men tend to be taller than women. Some writers probably try acting out the lines as they write them, and directors will sometimes intellectualise the themes of a play as they explore how to put it in front of an audience. Actors, of course, often talk relentlessly about their character to anyone who will listen, but the ways that writers, directors and actors like to express themselves *tend* to be in the ways I've described above.

So, if actors are able to convey human behaviour by tapping into the emotional truth of a character and just 'being', then it stands to reason that directors should exploit this talent during rehearsals. They should ask actors to get up and try things out as much as they can. Actors can't wait to get up on their feet. They know in their hearts that they will discover more by *doing* something than by talking about it too much. They trust their instincts. If they can just 'be' a character for a while, then they will discover how that character thinks and behaves – and they can do that through improvisation.

But before they start to improvise they have to be thoroughly prepared, and the place to start this preparation is the text of the play itself.

Looking for Clues

As all detectives know, you can't put a case together without at least a handful of clues to get you going. Similarly, you can't start improvising without knowing something about the play and the characters. So the first thing actors should do before anything else is to read the play. That's obvious. And then, less obviously, they should read it again. And then read it again. There are loads of clues in the text of a play, and it's surprising how much more an actor can discover on the second or third reading.

Unlike a novel, the text of a play contains very little in the way of descriptive material. There will possibly be a paragraph or two at the beginning to describe the set, or the way the writer imagines the stage will look, but after that, passages of descriptive text are few and far between. Some writers put in stage directions, like 'He pours himself a drink' or (famously, from *The Winter's Tale*) 'Exit, pursued by a bear', but most of the time these are just bits of action that the writer feels are vital to the plot and they don't really add much information. Playwrights also incorporate hints to persuade the actors to play the lines the way they want them to be played. Like 'Angrily', 'With a wry smile', 'With mounting annoyance', etc., but actually I've known many actors who will go through a script when they first get it and just cross these stage directions out. They feel that the playwright should write the dialogue, but the actor should discover how to play the scene for themselves.

So when an actor is trying to understand the action of a play, or starting to find out what their character is like, or attempting to fathom out how the characters feel about each other, most of the information can be found in the things the characters say and the way that they say them. In other words, the dialogue. That's where the clues, sometimes called the 'given circumstances', are to be found.

When actors first read a play, they are so concerned about their own 'part' that they often miss the subtleties of the plot. Ideally, an actor should read a play for the first time without knowing which part he or she will be playing. In that way they can get an overall view of the material without being distracted by the finer details of their character. This is not always possible, but it is desirable.

As they read the play, the actors should start gathering clues and writing them down. Even before rehearsals begin. These clues should be facts not speculations. 'I see this character with a wooden leg' may be an interesting idea, but if there is no reference to it in the text, then it is pure speculation. Rather like a detective finding an empty cigarette packet at the scene of the crime and then saying, 'I think the villain drove a Mercedes.' It may be true, but it's not very helpful in the early stages of an investigation unless it can be supported by facts.

'I have of late – but wherefore I know not – lost all my mirth,' says Hamlet to his friends Rosencrantz and Guildenstern. Of course he could be lying, but put it together with 'How weary, stale, flat, and unprofitable / Seem to me all the uses of this world,' which he says to himself, and 'I do not set my life at a pin's fee,' which he says to his best friend Horatio, then we begin to realise that Hamlet could be depressed. Or at least he thinks he's depressed. And that is something to start working on. An assumption fully supported by the text.

The villain may or may not have driven a Mercedes, but if a cigarette packet is found at the scene of the crime it's reasonable to assume that he or she could be a smoker.

First Reading

In rehearsals, the first reading of a play with the whole cast is a nerve-wracking experience. Some directors don't bother with a readthrough any more, but I think it's important, if only to settle everyone down. Often this is the first time that the actors will have met each other and it gives them the opportunity to relax a bit. Some of them will be a bit nervous of displaying their sight-reading skills in public so I usually make it a pretty light-hearted affair.

During this first readthrough, it is quite useful to stop at the end of each scene, section or act to have a discussion about what has been revealed. Again, these discussions should avoid speculation. People should only talk about things that can be supported by the information in the text. This way, everyone can share their observations and build up a catalogue of information and ideas.

When the readthrough is finished – and with all the pauses for discussion this may take all day or even longer – everyone should then discuss what the play is trying to say and what effect the author intended it to have on the audience. When a group gets deep into the rehearsal period it's very easy to lose sight of the basics and stop seeing the wood for the trees. After a first night I've often heard actors say things like 'I'd forgotten it was a comedy' or 'I didn't realise the play was so moving', so it's sensible in early stages to think about what a play is trying to achieve. Then everyone is working towards a shared objective.

Character Discussions

Having arrived at an understanding of the play as a whole, the next step is to discuss each of the characters. At this stage, the actors shouldn't get too precious about their own character. There will be a lot of creative and imaginative people in the room, and each actor should keep their minds open to other people's ideas. Other actors often come up with things that the actor playing a particular character may not have considered. Why not exploit this group creativity? Everyone benefits in the end.

If the rehearsal period is long enough, the whole cast can discuss each character, one at a time, but if not, the discussions can be in small groups comprised of actors whose characters are most likely to know things about each other: characters who are family members, or who are in the same scene together, characters who are best friends, characters who hate each other, etc.

These discussions should focus on collecting facts; however, there will be a certain amount of speculation. Some clues discovered in the text may *suggest* a fact rather than spelling it out. Yes, it's safe to say that Hamlet is depressed, but parts of the text could also suggest that he is jealous of Claudius's relationship with Gertrude (Hamlet's mother), or that he is still in love with his old girlfriend Ophelia, or that he is apprehensive about the sword fight with Laertes which happens in the last scene of the play. All these ideas are ripe for discussion, and everything should be written down for consideration at a later date.

Relationship Discussions

The cast should read the play together again, but this time everyone should think about the relationships between the characters in each scene. What do they think and feel about each other? How do their thoughts and feelings change throughout the course of the play? Again, it is a good idea to have a discussion with the whole cast after each scene, section or act while the ideas are still fresh in everyone's mind. And don't forget, even people who aren't actually in the scene may have interesting things to say because they will probably have a more objective view.

Having done that, people can then get into appropriate discussion groups to talk about relationships. The prime consideration in setting up these groups is to put characters together who would have met each other before the action of the play: characters that have a relationship, however tenuous. A servant who only has one line will have a relationship with the person they serve, so both actors need to find out what that is. A play about a family will need to have all the actors in the family getting together to discuss the interweaving and intricate relationships between each of them, in order to understand how some characters play people off against each other and others dominate, placate or counsel. But the most important consideration when setting up these groups is to put people together who are playing characters that bring some sort conflict to the play. If, for instance, you were rehearsing

Who's Afraid of Virginia Woolf? by Edward Albee, where the central characters are a middle-aged married couple who fight and argue and dig up the past for three solid acts, then the discussion between the actors playing George and Martha would be the main thrust of the relationship discussions and they could go on for a long time. That's fine, but at this stage the actors should still stick to the facts that are written in the play and not speculate. The other two characters, Nick and Honey, are a younger couple who have an equally complex and stressful marriage. They too will need in-depth discussions about the development of their relationship.

Who's Afraid of Virginia Woolf? is mainly about the relationship between George and Martha, but other plays will have a mixture of simple and complex relationships between many of the characters. Each of these relationships needs to be discussed by the actors playing the parts. If you are rehearsing *Hamlet*, for instance, then the actor playing Hamlet will need to get together with the actress playing his mother Gertrude, to discuss the relationship between these two characters; Polonius will have to have a discussion with his boss, the new king, Claudius; and Laertes will need to discuss his relationship with his sister Ophelia and with their father Polonius. But then Hamlet will also need to talk with Ophelia too because she is his ex-girlfriend, as will Polonius, her father. Gertrude will need to discuss things with her new husband Claudius but then she will also need to talk with Ophelia because at one time she was going to be Ophelia's mother-in-law. Rosencrantz should have a proper discussion with his mate Guildenstern, and they will both need to talk to Hamlet about how well they knew each other as students. The two gravediggers will obviously have to talk, and so too will Bernardo and Francisco who guard the battlements. It's a very complex play with a lot of interweaving subplots and this may sound like time-consuming, laborious work, but with careful planning some of these discussions can happen at the same time.

I usually set the actors up in pairs or small groups to have these discussions, and then I move from group to group so I can listen to what they are saying. In this way, the actors can discover things for themselves, while at the same time I can add my observations to the mix.

Although there can be three or four discussion groups happening at once, there will be times when some of the actors are not going to be involved in any of them. Hamlet has relationships with virtually all of the other characters in the play and will be going from group to group, but the gravediggers only know each other so after they have talked about their relationship they won't have anything else to do. When this happens I usually get those actors to join with other groups so they can bring an objective view to the discussion. After all, everyone is working on the same play and all opinions are useful.

The relationships between different characters is such an important aspect of any play that these discussions will probably continue on and off throughout the rehearsal process, but at this stage these group discussions will give the actors something to work with. In Chapter 6: Relationships, I describe a series of improvisations that will develop these character relationships even further, but the actors can't do that work until they have established a shared understanding of the basics.

The Social and Physical Environment of the Play

The final fact-finding discussion should be about the world that the characters inhabit. As before, these discussions should revolve around the clues in the text and not on speculation. When the actors start to improvise, they need to be fully supported by as much information as they can. Later on in the work they will be able to add their own imaginative interpretation to the factual evidence, but not at this stage. Unlike other rehearsal procedures, the actors use improvisation rather than intellectualisation to build upon the given circumstances, but before they start to improvise they need to build as clear and detailed a picture as they can. Remember, all these discussions are part of the preparation for *improvisation*, not the preparation for *performance*. That will come later.

So the actors need to understand where the play takes place. The actual environment. Is Elsinore (the castle in *Hamlet*) gloomy or cheerful? Is it full of people or is it rather deserted? What do the characters do with their leisure time? Are the lords and ladies friendly with the servants or do they treat them badly? Is Gertrude's bedroom vast and chilly or is it warm and cosy?

When we try to answer the questions about Elsinore, we must look to the text. Hamlet says:

> The King doth wake tonight and takes his rouse,
> Keeps wassail, and swagg'ring upspring reels,
> And, as he drains his draughts of Rhenish down,
> The kettle-drum and trumpet thus bray out
> The triumph of his pledge.

So we can assume that, despite Hamlet's gloomy mood, Elsinore is, at least now Claudius is in charge, Party Palace. Not a gloomy old castle with eerie silences and musty shadows, but rather a jolly place with lots of drinking and dancing and loud music.

However, the battlements must be pretty cold because Hamlet says, 'The air bites shrewdly; it is very cold.' And Horatio replies, 'It is a nipping and an eager air.' These are facts in the play about the environment and they can't be ignored. Although the chill in the air could be brought about by the imminent presence of a ghost rather than the time of year. In fact, they mention the cold so many times that it's worth considering whether it is *unnaturally* cold for the time of year. The battlements must be reasonably dark as well because right at the beginning of the play Bernardo says, 'Who's there?' and Francisco replies, 'Nay, answer me. Stand and unfold yourself.' Rather than making himself visible, Bernardo then says, 'Long live the King!' and Francisco answers with a question –

'Bernardo?' – which must mean he can't really see Bernardo properly, he just recognises his voice. So it's dark. Or perhaps it's misty! Which is it? All the characters must feel they are in the same environment so this issue should be resolved through discussion. The actors should talk about it. If they looked deeper into the text they would discover that it can't really be misty because later on Bernardo says:

> Last night of all
> When yond same star that's westward from the pole
> Had made his course t'illume that part of heaven
> Where now it burns…

'Yond same star,' he says, meaning he must be pointing at it, 'where now it burns' he says next, which must mean that he can see it. No mist. It must just be dark. And it's definitely cold, unnaturally so or not.

As you can see, a close examination of the text will reveal clues that indicate what the environment is like: it's easy for an actor to miss these clues if he or she isn't actually saying the lines. A detailed discussion with the whole group will not only bring these facts to light, but they will also create a unity of understanding, a shared springboard from which to dive into the depths of rehearsal. Get the basics established and identify all the given circumstances right at the start and there is plenty of time to look at the nuances later on through improvisation.

Final Group Readthrough

Having discussed the facts in the text – about the characters, their relationships and the environments that they inhabit – I would suggest that the actors have a final readthrough of the play just to mop up any clues that they might have missed and consolidate the ones they have discovered and discussed. They can go back to the text at any time to clarify any uncertainties, but for the next part of the rehearsal process the script itself can be set aside and everyone can venture into uncharted territory with all the equipment they need.

It's nearly time to improvise. I usually suggest that the actors start to learn their lines now, so when we eventually put the play on its feet, they don't have to rehearse with their scripts in their hands. Anyway, it's useful for them to keep a close eye on the actual text because their creativity and imagination can take the improvisations down some extraordinary paths that may not always be pertinent to the play. That's not really a problem since these inconsistencies can be ironed out later. But the director should be careful that the actors don't wander too far from the main objectives and facts of the play, otherwise the improvisations will not be so useful. The whole point of using improvisation in rehearsals is to make complex and in-depth discoveries about the characters and the play, not to create a whole new play.

2

Research

A few years ago I decided to study for a Masters degree so I would have some sort of qualification when I went in search of teaching work. I was already in my late forties and I had never studied anything properly, except when I went to drama school to study acting. And that wasn't the same thing at all. We didn't have to read books and write essays.

The degree was in Performance and it covered, amongst other things, gender issues, mixed media, outreach and performance art. But the module that I found most interesting was about postmodernism.

Before doing the course I'd heard that word bandied about, naturally, but it was hard to find anyone who could explain what it meant. Or perhaps no one had the time. Or more likely – hardly anyone knew!

Two things attracted me to the postmodernism module in the early stages. The first was the fact that our main tutor – Patrick Campbell – seemed to have a wry smile flickering around his lips as he talked about 'metanarratives', 'fragmentation', 'eclecticism', 'pastiche' and 'the self-seeing self'. He seemed to find the subject amusing. But what eventually clinched my interest was a lecture that Signey Henderson gave called 'Postmodernism and the Theatre' which she started off by saying:

'I can't make up my mind whether theatre has always been postmodern, or by its very definition, can never be.'

Right. The lecturer doesn't even know what postmodernism is. We're onto something here.

In fact, it turns out that the subject is a quagmire of conflicting theories and philosophies. I had to read all sorts of books, some of which were very heavy-going. I took notes. I filled folders with quotes and pictures. I wrote ideas on multicoloured filing cards, tagged, numbered and organised. I talked about postmodernism with my friends, although only one of them was interested, and that was because he had studied it at art school. Funnily enough, when we discussed the subject, he had the same wry smile playing about his lips as Patrick Campbell. What is it about postmodernism that makes people smile like that?

My dissertation set out to demonstrate that the truest postmodern moment in British theatre was when an actor corpses (laughs unintentionally and uncontrollably) during the performance of a pantomime. And you know what? I found I started to develop a wry smile as I was writing it. I was becoming a true aficionado of postmodernism.

And what about all those coloured filing cards and all that research? Did I manage to cram everything into my dissertation? Well, not really. Some of it. A bit of it. Enough to impress the examiners. But no. Not all of it by any means. So had all that research been necessary? Yes. Definitely. Without it I would never have even considered that the British pantomime was a suitable subject for discussion. I would never have been able to analyse the symbiotic relationship between the audience and the cast when an actor corpses. I would never have been able to make interesting connections and links between British pantomime and heavy-duty French philosophising. I would never have been able to write my dissertation because the subject would not have embedded itself so firmly into my subconscious.

All that background knowledge was essential.

ALTHOUGH AN EXAMINATION AND ANALYSIS OF THE TEXT is crucial before you can start improvising, it is also very important to research the background of the play you are working on. Actors need to know the world which their characters inhabit. They need to know the social customs of the period. They need to know the mood and rhythm of the era in which the play is set. They need to know the prevailing political climate. They need to know what their characters would wear, and how their furniture would look. They need to know the weight and feel of everyday objects and they need to be able to imagine using them. The more knowledge they have about the background of the play, the more confident they will feel during an improvisation.

Allocating Research

Research is very time-consuming. The actors will have to browse libraries, surf the internet, read books and watch DVDs. And since time is of the essence during the rehearsal period it is probably sensible to allot different research tasks to different actors. One actor can be getting information about the playwright and his contemporaries while another is searching for pictures of the period to find out what sort of clothes people wore or what their houses might have looked like. With individuals or small groups working on different aspects of research, they can refine their discoveries and feed them back to the rest of the cast.

These feedback sessions can happen in a number of ways, depending on the available rehearsal time. The best way (and the most fun) is for small groups to devise some sort of feedback presentation. This can be in the form of a fifteen- to twenty-minute show with costumes, props, dialogue, puppets or whatever the group can think of. If the presentation of research information is entertaining, it is often more memorable. The next best form of feedback is when the research findings are simply read out to the cast. This can culminate in a question and answer session and information can be shared in a group discussion. Finally, if there is limited time, the results of the research can be printed out and distributed to the cast so they will be able to read it in their own time.

The Playwright

Before working on a play it is advisable to find out as much about the playwright as possible in order to get a better understanding of the writer's themes and interests. With well-known playwrights there may be numerous, in-depth biographies either in book form or on the internet, but even with less-well-known playwrights it is usually possible to find out some information about their lives. Writers often use their own life experience as part of the creative process, so if the actors understand the writer they will often get a better understanding of the motivations and obsessions of the characters they write about.

Of course, you may be working on a new play by a first-time writer, so this sort of research is impossible, but at least you might be able to find out where the playwright was born or what sort of education he or she had. The best-case scenario is if the writer is in rehearsals with you because you can engage him or her in conversation and ask loads of questions.

If you are rehearsing a play by a reasonably well-known playwright, the actors should also read other plays by the same writer. Again, recurring themes, similar characters and comparable relationships can often give a deeper insight into the particular play being rehearsed: the faded beauty who occurs in several of Tennessee Williams's plays; the problems with communication that Harold Pinter explores in much of his work; the impending decay and destruction of society that lies at the heart of Chekhov's writing. If actors read other plays by the same author it can give them a much broader picture of the playwright's main themes and preoccupations and it should help them create more complex characters.

And, of course, the actors should read plays by other playwrights of the period in order to get a better understanding of
the theatrical climate of the times.

The more the actors know before they start, the better
equipped they will be to fulfil the playwright's objectives and
present an informed and comprehensive version of the play.

The Playwright's Intentions

Most playwrights that have stood the test of time were trying
to alter their audience's expectations. They were cutting edge,
innovative and sometimes shocking at the time their plays were
first produced, so if you want to give the audience a similar
experience, it is essential to understand the prevailing theatrical conventions of the era in which a play was written. How did
the audience feel on the first night of *Hamlet* when Bernardo
walked onto an empty stage in broad daylight and said, 'Who's
there?' and Francisco replied, 'Nay, answer me: stand, and
unfold yourself.' These are the opening lines of the play. Before
that particular first night (afternoon), audiences were used to
some sort of prologue before the play began. An actor walked
to the front of the stage and explained what the play was going
to be about: 'Two households both alike in dignity...' (*Romeo
and Juliet*) or 'O for a muse of fire, that would ascend / The
brightest heaven of invention...' (*Henry V*). Or if there wasn't
a prologue, at least the opening lines would be in verse, and
spoken by a character with status: a nobleman or a king. 'Now
is the winter of our discontent...' says Richard III. 'Hence!
home, you idle creatures, get you home...' says Flavius at the
beginning of *Julius Caesar*. Before *Hamlet* was first performed,
the audience expected to be taken firmly by the hand by an
important character and led clearly into the story. But what
was this? Two apparently low-life characters speaking in prose
and not being able to recognise each other. The first line is only
two syllables long and it's not even in verse. The two characters
challenge each other to identify themselves. It must have been

a dynamic experience for the audience, and Shakespeare was obviously trying to unsettle them from the very start.

So if it was Shakespeare's intention to unsettle the audience, then that will give some indication as to how the actors playing Bernardo and Francisco might perform the scene. They will understand that the opening of the play should be mysterious or even confusing for the audience.

If the actors understand the writer's intentions, then they will be better equipped to serve the play. Was the writer trying to shock the audience or to entertain them? Did the writer want to make the audience think about the human condition, or educate and politicise them? Was the writer trying to make the audience laugh or cry? It's important to know these things in order to understand how to perform the play.

The Period

Productions of Shakespeare's plays are often set in different periods of history and in different countries. I've seen *Twelfth Night* set in colonial India, *Coriolanus* set in medieval Japan, and *Macbeth* set practically everywhere from 1920s Chicago to war-torn Bosnia. People also update classics by other playwrights. There have been modern-dress productions of Sheridan, Wilde, Chekhov, Pirandello and many others. So when researching various aspects of the period, rather than thinking about the time the *play was written*, the actors should consider the period in which the *production is set*. Sometimes these will be one and the same, but there is no point in researching Elizabethan England, or even Verona, when you are going to set *Romeo and Juliet* in the slums of modern-day Bangkok.

In order to keep this clear distinction, I often refer to *the production* rather than *the play* throughout this book.

Visual Research

Pictures, pictures, pictures! An enormous amount of information can be gathered by looking at pictures of the period. Photographs, paintings, films, sketches, etc. By gathering together as much visual research as possible, the actors will get a clear impression of their character's surroundings and the clothing they would wear. They'll also know which household items would have been in use and they'll know what the furniture looked like. They will have an idea of what these things are made of and in some cases they will know how various appliances work and what they do. These visual images will help them appreciate how objects might feel in their hands, how their clothes might make them look and how their environment might impact on their character.

Transport, Furniture and Fashion

The objects that surround us have a strong influence on the way we behave. If we are used to having a car, we tend to be able to rush from place to place, deal with things quickly and move on. If, however, we have to walk everywhere, then we know that a certain amount of time has to be allotted to a journey, and consequently travel becomes a time for thinking. If the roads are busy with traffic, pedestrians need to be more alert than they are when taking a relaxing stroll through the countryside. A horse ride can be exhausting. A journey by train can become a social event. Modes of transport from the period in which the production is set are important for an actor. When their character enters a room, they should know exactly how they got there because it could easily affect their character's mood and rhythm.

The furniture that the characters use will also have an effect on the way they behave. Hard wooden benches are very different from beanbags. A sofa is different from a wing-backed chair. These things not only look different but they influence the way that people sit in them and the way they move around in them, and that will affect a character's physicality. Ultimately, the designer should produce the appropriate furniture for the actors to use during the performance, but forewarned is forearmed and if the actors know what to expect they will be able to start making adjustments early on.

The clothes that people wear in any period of history will also have an effect on the way they behave. During the flamboyant extravagances of the Restoration period, men liked to display a finely turned calf muscle and women liked to flaunt their cleavage but keep their legs totally hidden. The androgynous flapper from the twenties ensured her breasts were firmly flattened. The asexual, skinny male hippie from the sixties boasted more luxuriant hair than his girlfriend. The prevailing attitudes and customs of the time influence the clothes that people choose to wear and that has a big influence on, not only how they look, but how they feel. There's a lot to be learnt from the fashions of any particular period.

There are many illustrated books about clothing through the ages and the internet is a useful resource for information and pictures. If you are able to get to the Victoria and Albert Museum in London they have a fantastic collection of male and female clothing that covers four centuries of European fashionable dress, from the beginning of the eighteenth century to the latest creations of the twenty-first century.

The Importance of Being Earnest by Oscar Wilde

In late-nineteenth-century England, the upper classes would be transported from place to place, either by a horse-drawn carriage, or by train. If they were travelling with someone else, this sort of transport would give them lots of time to talk, so they'd become used to speaking in well-constructed sentences, using conversation as an entertainment in itself, and listening to each other in order to be entertained.

The interiors of upper-class houses at the time would have hard wooden floors with carpets placed in the middle of the room. No fitted carpets, of course, so the characters would have had to be careful how they walked about. Leather-soled shoes could easily slip on polished wooden floors. The edge of the carpet could trip them up. Caution was required at all times. The furniture at the time was formal and uncomfortable. It would have been quite difficult to lounge around or slump on Victorian chaises longues. Dining chairs were stiff and hard-backed, whilst writing tables were small and delicate. All this would affect the physicality of the characters.

The clothes of the period were tight and formal and they produced a tight and formal way of behaving. Men's suits and women's dresses were often made in rather light colours and cut from expensive cloth. In fact, the clothing that the characters wore at the time of *The Importance of Being Earnest* would not have been cheap, so it had to be looked after. There were no dry-cleaners, so people had to be careful not to get their clothes dirty or creased. This would have produced a certain amount of caution about sitting down, or walking around outside.

Weather

It's simple really – maybe a bit too obvious – but if it's really hot, it can slow you down and heat your passions, and if it's really cold it can make you tense and isolated. When there's a blustering wind it can make you feel insecure and nervous and continual rain can make you depressed. Generalisations, I know, but useful tendencies. Think about the setting for *Romeo and Juliet*. Italy in the summer is often warm and dry. When the characters are walking the streets of Verona the hot sun will affect the way they move. There is a particular way of ambling that people employ in hot countries to conserve energy. The brightness of the sun will affect their vision and the heat of it could make them quick to quarrel. On the other hand, the wet and windy Scottish highlands could make the characters in plays such as *Macbeth* feel insecure and depressed.

Then there are the seasons. The optimism of spring, the lazy days of summer, the sense of decay that autumn brings and the bleak, bleak midwinter: sharp, biting and energising.

Codes of Conduct and Acceptable Behaviour

Social customs and recreational activities vary enormously from place to place and at different times in history. I've often experienced an uncertainty about how to behave when I have been travelling abroad, particularly when I've travelled far afield. Middle-Eastern countries, Far-Eastern countries, South American countries: the social customs are all very different. Of course, a human being is a human being, but the way people behave is often governed by the prevailing mores of the time and place and if you get it wrong you can look ridiculous or even appear to be insulting.

And it's not only long-distance travel that throws up these differences. Go to another part of your own country and you will discover cultural variations. Even visiting another part of your own city where there may be immigrant communities can make you feel out of place because you don't know the correct codes of conduct.

Then there are different periods of history. How did people make social contact with a stranger four hundred years ago? How about one hundred years ago? Or even twenty years ago? Things are changing all the time. What did people do in the evening before television was invented? What did they do before books? What sports did they play? What games? When I was a young actor with the Royal Shakespeare Company there was a joke that if you were supposed to be hanging out with nothing to do during a scene, you would ask the props department for a cup and ball. And how often do we see children in Victorian drama playing with a hoop? We know about these activities, but there must have been lots more. You get bored of the cup and ball after a while. The hoop only keeps you entertained for a limited period. So what else did people do?

Then there is they way you greet a stranger. Or the way you greet a friend. Do you say 'Hi!' or do you say 'What cheer?' Do you bear-hug and slap each other's backs or do you air-kiss three times? Do you bow from the waist? Do you share a high five? Do you keep your hat on or sweep it across the ground before a stranger's feet? Do you keep your gloves on when you shake hands? Do you snap your heels together?

I could go on and on.

How do members of the opposite sex treat each other? There are a great many subtle differences there. How does someone treat a servant? How does a servant treat the master? Should children be seen and not heard? Do you flirt with another man's wife?

There is a lot to be discovered about social behaviour and accepted customs and in order to present a believable version of a specific period these things need to be understood.

But it isn't so easy to discover how people actually behaved in the past. Books, pictures and the internet will help, but one of the things that I find most useful for this sort of exploration is to listen to music from the period or the cultural environment in which a production is set. Music is great for stirring the imagination, and it has always been part of the social structure of communities. People like to listen to music together. They like to interact with each other by dancing to music and they like to use music to entertain each other. Try playing a love scene to the accompaniment of a lute and then play the same scene listening to Tchaikovsky's *Romeo and Juliet*. The lute has a delicacy and gentle sweetness which expresses an idealised version of pure love, whereas Tchaikovsky's music sweeps you through magnificent emotional soundscapes with a transcending release of pent-up passion. I would suggest the different styles of music from these different periods of history symbolise the prevailing feelings about love.

Political Climate

It's all very well acting out a domestic drama but what is going on in the outside world? Is there a war raging overseas that might be endangering the lives of your children? Are you rich when the rest of your local community is living on the breadline? Are you living in a repressive society or is there an optimistic attitude to life in your community? Have you 'never had it so good' or are there 'reds under the bed'?

We are all affected by the society in which we live and the way we are governed, however much we take it for granted or try not to think about it. In fact, the political climate of our own time seems to us to be quite normal. So when an actor is playing a character who lives in another period of history or in another part of the world, they must understand and appreciate their character's world until it seems quite natural to them. The characters in Chekhov's plays, for example, who seem to be reasonably relaxed and comfortable (albeit a little depressed), are surrounded by a climate of massive social unrest which leads to the tension and depth of subtext in the plays. If the actors don't have a full understanding of the political climate of that particular time, they won't feel the constant pressure and uncertainty that is a major element of Chekhov's plays. While Hamlet is confused and depressed, or Richard III is pathologically ambitious, the rest of the country is optimistic and celebratory. As are the people of Scotland when Macbeth sets out on his murderous quest. The prevailing political climate underpins the plot and motivates the characters' actions.

The more information that the actors can find out about the political and social events surrounding the time of the production, the better. Was it a time of prolonged peace? Who was in power? What did the general populous feel about the society they lived in? Were people living through good times or bad? Was there fighting in the streets? Was it a time of prosperity and happiness? These are the sort of questions that need to be addressed.

Thematic Research

Some plays have particular themes that can be the subject of wider research. For instance, *The Colour of Justice*, which was originally devised and edited by Richard Norton-Taylor for London's Tricycle Theatre, is based on the transcripts of the Stephen Lawrence Inquiry. Stephen Lawrence was a black teenager who was killed in an unprovoked racial attack in 1993. The inquiry found that there was 'institutional racism' in the Metropolitan Police. If you were working on this play, it would be informative to examine the history of racism in Britain; the recruitment and training of the police force; the British legal system; and the social environment of South East London at the end of the twentieth century.

Similarly, if you were working on Shakespeare's *Measure for Measure* it would be helpful to research the law and forms of justice at the time that the production is set, as well as the pre-vailing attitudes to sex before marriage, and how women fitted into society four hundred years ago when Shakespeare wrote the play.

The Laramie Project by Moisés Kaufman is about a real-life homophobic murder in Wyoming in 1998 and its effect on the local community, so it would be important for all the actors to understand how the people of Wyoming felt about homosexuality at the time of the murder.

Later in the book I describe a series of improvisations to explore the themes in *Someone Who'll Watch Over Me* by Frank McGuinness. For this play, the actors need to understand what it might be like to be unfairly kidnapped and imprisoned; how people behave when they are isolated and at the mercy of violent men; and what effects boredom and hopelessness have on the human spirit. In order to prepare for those improvisations it would be important for the cast to research these themes so they have a strong understanding of them before they explore their characters' reactions.

Further Research

There is always room for further research, but that will depend on the circumstances of the production. If the play is set in a courtroom, then the reality of that world needs to be understood. If a character works on a farm, that needs to be researched. If a character has a physical disability, or is suffering from psychological problems, then the truth about how that affects his or her life has to be examined. Every play is different and will have different research requirements. Every character is different and likewise there will be specific areas of research to suit each and every character in each and every play. It would be impossible to list all the research requirements that may be needed when working on a production, but the broad examples discussed above are good starting points and will be valuable in most circumstances.

The important thing to realise about research is that nothing should be taken for granted. The true facts should be discovered, considered and ultimately embedded into the creative psyche of the actors so they can inhabit their characters' world clearly and naturally when they are improvising. Of course, research is an important part of any rehearsal process and will ultimately bring truth and clarity to a production, but when you are going to use improvisation as a rehearsal tool, a thorough understanding of all aspects of the period will underpin the actors' imaginative explorations.

—

It seems like there is a lot of hard work to do before getting down to the creative 'fun' of exploring through improvisation. The play has to be read and reread. The text has to be examined with a fine-tooth comb to extract as many clues as possible. The actors have to discuss what they have discovered without inventing anything that isn't supported by the text. They have to research as much information as they can, and they have to share the results of their research with everyone else. But having done all this they will now be ready. Their parachutes are packed. The plane is in flight. All the safety procedures are in place and they know how to land. Their helmets are secured and their goggles in place. The door is open. The wind rushes past. Now all they have to do is jump out of the plane and soar confidently through the air like eagles in flight.

3

Background
Improvisations

I've always enjoyed watching Wimbledon on television. I used to play tennis when I was younger, before I smashed up my right arm in a car accident, so I know the subtleties of the game quite well. The scoring system in tennis is the most wonderful device for creating tension and excitement. I've no idea how it came about, with its 'fifteen-love' and 'game, set and match point', but it really works. Two players can have been going at it hammer and tongs for a couple of hours and then get to a point in the match where one of them is about to become the victor. He serves wide; his opponent returns a cross-court pass and the potential victor miss-hits the ball and loses the point. Two hours of tough tennis later his opponent serves an ace on match point and becomes the champion. What an upset.

Tennis players, like all sportsmen, prepare like mad for competitions. They train and exercise and practise. Especially the sportsmen who become champions. They are totally one-track about it all. But the interesting thing about a sport like tennis, where one person is in direct competition with another, is that the champions never get to practise or train with people who can beat them so they are not used to losing, and they can never properly practise the tension and drama of a challenging competition. They can work on their serve. They can analyse and discuss tactics with their coach. They can talk endlessly with a sports psychologist. They can exercise in the gym and they can play hours of tennis with lesser players. In fact, they can prepare mentally and physically day and night. They can train and analyse. They can eat the right food and get the right amount of rest. But they can't practise a championship tennis match until they are actually playing it.

And, of course, championship matches are what they live for.

That's when they are totally focused and that is why they train. They learn more about themselves and the quality of their tennis when they are playing in tournaments than they do at any time in practise.

Let's face it, no matter how much they train, professional tennis players are at their best when they are in important competitions. They'd be nowhere without preparation, but in the end it's playing under pressure that counts. That's when they are 'in the moment'. That's when they truly discover how to play championship tennis.

That's because they learn the most when they are actually doing what they do best.

W HEN ACTORS ARE IMPROVISING, THEY ARE 'IN THE moment' exactly like tennis players in a championship tennis match. They will have prepared as thoroughly as possible by reading the play, researching the playwright, looking at pictures, reading books, surfing the internet and sharing information with each other. Now they can do what they do best. Through improvisation, they can start to experience the world of their play and make discoveries by using their own creativity and skill.

Rules of Improvisation

As I said in the Introduction, when improvisation is used as a rehearsal tool, the actors should never feel the pressure to entertain. All they have to do is be truthful to their character and keep themselves open and receptive to whatever may happen. They should try to imagine the environment in which the improvisation takes place, and they should make sure they know their character's objectives and emotions before they start. Since these improvisations are all about making new discoveries, there should be little or no pre-planning beyond setting up the scenario clearly and then just letting the improvisation unfold.

Stop Self-censorship

Not everything that actors do or say in an improvisation will turn out to be valuable, or even be true to the production, but that doesn't matter. It is far more important for the actors to go with the flow of an improvisation and let it develop naturally, however bizarrely. If they continually try to analyse and censor their creativity during an improvisation, then they will become inhibited and tentative, and not learn anything new. I've often seen actors stop an improvisation because 'it's not going right', but to my mind that is indicative of self-censorship and will block any new discoveries. They are not allowing themselves to go into unexplored territory because it scares them. And how can they learn like that? Anything that veers from the path of prior knowledge can be useful. New things can be learned, some of them may be inappropriate, but others will be exciting and informative. If an improvisation goes completely off-track, it doesn't matter. The inaccuracies can be a useful point of discussion when the improvisation has finished. In that way the apparently 'wrong' discoveries become productive and interesting, and the 'right' discoveries will be exciting, original and unique.

Group Improvisations

When a group of actors start to explore a play through improvisation, their knowledge and understanding will be rather limited and that can make them a bit insecure, so I usually start with generalised group improvisations to help everyone get the feel of the larger world in which the production is set. I will often ask the actors to abandon the characters they will be playing and create new ones. For this they can be anyone they like, as long as their new character is appropriate to the period. I find it best to make these improvisations fun and straightforward so that the actors get used to working together and start to trust each other.

The Street

Life happens on the street. No matter where you live or what you do, sometime or another you have to walk down a street. Even the idle rich living on their country estates will sometimes visit the town to stroll along the shopping boulevards. And all these streets, roads and avenues are quite different, some of them are crowded and full of life and some of them are quiet and empty. They could be narrow thoroughfares hemmed in by tall buildings or they could be wide, shady avenues. They could smell disgusting and oppressive or the air could waft with the sweet smell of flowers. They could be dusty and uneven with an open drain running down the middle or they could be modern tarmacked roads with heavy traffic. But whatever the streets are like, you can be pretty sure that the characters in the play will have walked down them recently. Maybe even just before they entered a scene. Walking in the street will have been an experience that will have been shared by most of the characters in the play.

Street-life Exercise

Start this group exercise by asking all the actors to imagine that they themselves are walking down a street. They shouldn't be their characters at this stage, they should just be themselves. If the production is set in another time or in another culture, they will have to imagine that they themselves are of that time or of that culture and see how it affects the way they move and their view of the world.

To start with they should imagine that they are on their own. They may be aware of other people in the room, but they should just ignore them as if they were strangers.

Once the actors are walking, start to describe the street, road or path they are walking down by using the information that has been gathered through research. If they have seen pictures of streets with trees planted along the sidewalk, then ask them to imagine those trees. Imagine how they look. Imagine how the sun shines through the leaves and imagine the way they smell. If the production takes place in a medieval town, then ask the actors to imagine the uneven quarry stones or the cobbles. Ask them to imagine the way the buildings form canyons that press in on the narrow alleys. Ask them to imagine the smell of raw sewage and the sound of dogs barking. Using sensory input, describe as many sights, sounds and smells as possible so the actors can immerse themselves in that world. Are the streets crowded? Then let the other actors be the crowd, and jostle past each other. Are they empty? Then let them imagine how a passing stranger might disturb their solitude.

Street-life Improvisation

Once the actors have explored the above exercise on their own, ask them to get into small groups of maybe two or three people, and then suggest that they create some sort of relationships. Are they lovers or are they a family? Are they colleagues from work or are they neighbours just passing the time together? If the street would have a market, then a couple of people could have stalls. If there is likely to be a police presence, ask someone to be a police officer. Whatever seems appropriate.

Once everyone has a role, let the group start the street-life improvisation. It's usually a good idea to allow these group improvisations to last for about fifteen minutes, so the actors have the time to experience the world that they, as a group, are creating.

Afterwards there should be a group discussion so that each actor can share their discoveries and experiences.

📖 *The Merchant of Venice* by William Shakespeare

The Rialto is a bridge in Venice that has shops built along the sides. It has long been a place for Venetians to gather in the evening and pass the time. In fact, it is still very common for Italians to appear in small groups at the end of the day and just hang out in the street to gossip and chat. In *The Merchant of Venice,* one of the characters asks, 'What news on the Rialto?', so that would be a sensible starting point for a street-life improvisation. With the proper research, the actors should have a clear mental image of the environment and the sort of characters who may be on the streets, so bringing this world to life will give them a solid basis for various scenes that take place in the street during the production.

⚡ Street-life Improvisations in Character

Street-life improvisations can also be used later in rehearsals when the actors have created their characters and their characters have developed relationships with other characters. In this case, of course, the actors would be improvising as the characters they are playing in the production. This is particularly useful for plays that are partially or wholly set in the street and have crowd scenes in them, like *Julius Caesar* by William Shakespeare, *Street Scene* by Elmer Rice or *Balm in Gilead* by Lanford Wilson.

> *A View from the Bridge* by Arthur Miller
>
> Arthur Miller's play is set in Brooklyn, a borough of New York, and it shows how cramped living conditions and the stress of relationships can make you feel isolated and alone. The characters in the play live in a tight-knit, supportive community and the actors need to understand how this community works in order to incorporate the underlying sense of group security into their performance.
>
> Coney Island is an amusement park in Brooklyn and is exactly the sort of place where the characters in the play would go for a fun day out. It is easy to research Coney Island on the internet to find out what it looked like and how it might feel to be there. Having done that, all the actors, as their characters, can improvise a holiday weekend visit to Coney Island amusement park. For this improvisation, the characters who are friends or relations in the play should decide whether they would go as a group, in couples or whether they would go alone. Whatever seems right to them. Once they are improvising, of course, they can talk to anyone they like, but they must only 'know' the people that their characters in the play would know.

Social Dances

Music is a great stimulus for the imagination and with a certain amount of research it is possible to improvise a suitable social dance for the period or the culture in which the production is set. Many actors have some experience of period dances, but if not they can a least fake some sort of appropriate dance steps. And the music will help. A waltz has a very simple basis, and although the jitterbug may have a complex collection of movements both solo and in pairs, once the music is playing then a simple jive would be enough. The charleston, the gavotte, the sixties' drug-induced solo exploration of self-expression: most actors will give these things a shot. Of course, if there is a dance teacher or a choreographer to hand, then they can spend half an hour or so teaching a few basic steps.

The whole ritual of asking someone for a dance, that person deciding to accept, and then both people dancing together often symbolises the way that members of the opposite sex relate to each other at a particular period of history. The whole thing usually starts with an invitation. The immortal line in my parents' day was: 'May I have the pleasure of the next dance?' In more formal times the ladies would carry a little notebook with them and the gentlemen would 'book' a dance for a particular part of the evening. Even when the male request became less formal, as it was when I was young, it still had the same sentiment. 'Wanna dance?' or even 'OK?' would be the opening gambit. Nowadays there doesn't seem to be any request, more of an unspoken mutual agreement. And people don't just dance in pairs any more, they dance in groups, or in same-sex pairs, and the ritual courtship that used to be so formal has now become subtle and free-flowing.

When two people are dancing together it can be quite an intimate experience and the way that they hold each other has changed considerably over the years. There have been times when men and women touched only by the tips of their fingers. At other times they have held each other carefully at arm's length, with one hand on a shoulder, perhaps, or just touching the waist, and the bodies kept well away from each other. Then for my parents' generation it was the fashion for men and women to hold each other extremely closely as they danced rather formal waltzes and foxtrots, guiding each other around the dance floor with their stomachs pressed tight. My generation often didn't touch at all. Both people would face each other and try to dance empathetically. It was a question of improvising movements in such a way that there was a physical harmony between the two of you. Each person trying to take on the style of their partner as they danced.

The tango has always appeared to be incredibly sexual, as has Spanish flamenco and the Apache dances of the Paris Left Bank. So much so that these dances have often been used to symbolise the sex act itself in films and in the theatre. Spanish dancing seems to represent a battle for supremacy. Apache dancing represents the relationship between a prostitute and a pimp. The tango symbolises mutual sexual passion. In some cultures, representational dances tell stories of unrequited love, or a battle between tribes, or the movements and mating rituals of various animals and birds.

Dance can be many things. Ritual. Performance. Storytelling. Art. Spiritual expression. And it has formed a large part of the lives of people in all periods of history and in all cultures. While these formalised or ritual group dances have often represented an expression of solidarity within the community, social dances are usually an expression of the cultural mores and codes of conduct of the period. As such, it is possible to explore both of these things through social dance improvisations.

Social Dance Improvisation

With research it is possible to identify the popular dance music of both the period of the production and/or the social environment in which the production is set. First of all, the cast should get in the mood by dancing as themselves to the music that is going to be used for the improvisation. To start with, they can dance in any way they like, but after a while they should start to dance in a style that suits the music and is an approximation of the actual dance steps. If there is a choreographer present or someone in the group that has some knowledge of the dance, then the cast can learn a few basic moves.

Then there should be a discussion about the accepted social behaviour of the period or culture. The actors can share their knowledge of manners and customs so that everyone has some idea of how to behave.

Finally, everyone should create characters and relationships which are appropriate to the style of the production as they did for the *Street-life Improvisation*. At this stage it is best that they don't use the characters from the play because they won't know enough about them yet.

This extended improvisation has three or four distinct stages and these should be described to the actors before they start. However, once the improvisation is underway, it should unfold without any interruption from the director, apart from an indication of when to move from stage to stage. The music should be playing throughout.

Preamble

Depending on the period of the production, there can be a preamble when the male and female members of the cast form two different gender groups and improvise a discussion about their hopes and fears of the forthcoming dance.

Invitation to Dance

The next part of the improvisation involves inviting someone to dance. Depending on the play, each of the male members of the cast should ask one of the female members to dance using the appropriate dance invitation of the period, and the female cast member should accept in a similar way.

The Dance

The next part of the improvisation is the dance itself. Again, depending on the period, people should see if they can have conversations while they dance.

The Outcome

The final part of the improvisation should be whatever happens after the dance has finished. Maybe the couple want to continue their conversation quietly in the corner of the room, or maybe each person wants to go back to their gender group to tell everyone what has happened. Or it could be that one of the pair wants to dance with a different person and sets about trying to make that happen, while the other is depressed and lonely. As long as the actors stay in the style of the production, they can experiment and explore as much as they like.

As with the *Street-life Improvisation*, this improvisation can either be used in early stages of rehearsal with everyone inventing a character or later in rehearsals when the actors can improvise a social dance as their characters from the play.

Period of Adjustment by Tennessee Williams

This play is set in America during the 1950s and it involves two male characters who have fought together in the Korean War and two female characters who are their wives. One couple are newlyweds, the other couple have been married for five years and the play is about the pains and difficulties of both their relationships.

In the middle of the twentieth century, the social and sexual interaction between men and women was very different from how it became fifty years later. The sexual revolution hadn't started and most women weren't 'liberated'. Consequently there were many misunderstandings about the opposite sex. If you look at the dances of the time – the jitterbug, the lindy hop or the jive – you will see that the man was the dominant partner, often throwing the woman around like a rag doll, while he strutted and controlled the movements of the dance. On the other hand, during the invitation-to-dance ritual, the woman was put on a pedestal and, although she couldn't initiate anything by asking the man to dance, she certainly had the power to accept or refuse the invitation.

Using the music of people like Cab Calloway, Louis Jordan, The Andrews Sisters and The Ink Spots, the actors should be able to approximate the dance style. If the man takes control and spins the woman around whenever he pleases, the actors will get the right feel for the dance. The music will help them all to create the right atmosphere and the correct form of social interaction, and the whole improvisation will help the actors understand the way the sexes felt about each other at that time.

Status

A funny thing happened to me years ago. Just after I left drama school I had an audition for a small part in Richard Attenborough's film *A Bridge Too Far*. He needed loads of young actors to play the soldiers. Not exactly extras, because he wanted to be able to give these actors lines whenever necessary, but at this stage there were no particular parts.

There were hundreds of us in the room.

After Attenborough explained everything to us like a general mustering his troops, we had to parade one by one in front of him while he gave each of us a cursory glance and said either 'Officer' and sent us to the left side of the room, or 'Private' and sent us to the right. He didn't talk to us. He just cast us by the way we looked.

I was never in the movie, but some of my friends were and they had a great time. They told me a funny story. Apparently, when all these young actors were in their costumes, some dressed as officers and some as privates, and they were waiting around on the set with nothing to do, the ones dressed as privates would sit on the ground playing cards and smoking cigarettes while the ones dressed as officers would stand upright with their hands clasped behind their backs and talk seriously about matters of great importance.

'The apparel oft proclaims the man,' says Polonius in *Hamlet*, and he's right. The actors were cast by their appearance but the clothes gave them their status.

Actors and directors are familiar with status conflicts: when you work on a play there are a lot of them going on in the rehearsal room. Sometimes a high-status character only has a few lines because the play is about low-status people. So in the hierarchy of the rehearsal room, high-status *actors* (the experienced ones with the biggest parts) may be playing low-status *characters* – like servants – who, during the course of the play, have to defer to a detective or a countess being played by an actor in his or her first job with only a few lines in Act Three. It's not too hard for an experienced actor to be able to act a lower-status character in front of an inexperienced actor, but it is sometimes quite hard for the newcomer to properly inhabit the authority that is needed for the part when he or she may be in awe of their more experienced colleague.

Status Improvisations

If an actor is finding it hard to play the correct status of their character, then they can be asked to explore that particular status in an improvisation. Some people find it hard to be a high-status person and some people find it hard to be low-status. Sometimes, in the hierarchy or the workplace or social group, a person will have to defer to someone higher up while at the same time they have status over someone lower down. A head waiter, for instance, will treat his customers with a great deal of deferential respect, but he will also be in charge of his staff so he will have to demand a similar sort of respect from them. These things are not easy to play if you aren't used to them.

A few years ago I was directing *The Vortex* by Noël Coward and the actor playing Pawnie was having trouble with the role. Pawnie is an older character who could be straight out of a Restoration comedy like *The School for Scandal* by Sheridan. When he speaks he 'takes the stage', as it were, and makes beautiful, bitchy pronouncements to anyone who may be listening. He doesn't care who he offends and his turns of phrase are immaculate and refined. He entertains his friends with his cutting wit and sharp observation, like Oscar Wilde or Quentin Crisp. He's camp, adorable and dangerous.

The trouble is that the actor playing Pawnie wasn't like that at all. He had no idea how to say a line with the confident assumption that everyone would think he was witty, so he backed away from the lines and tended to mumble them.

In order to help him overcome this problem, I set up an improvisation where the actor, as himself, simply had to tell the rest of the cast what he did in the morning from the moment he woke up. While he did this the rest of the cast had to sit at his feet, gaze adoringly up at him and react as if everything he said was a brilliant witticism. They could encourage him, clap, laugh, anything they liked, but they had to adore him.

'The alarm went off at eight o'clock.'

'Oh marvellous!' Clap, clap, clap. 'What happened next?'

'I put on my dressing gown and went downstairs to the kitchen.'

'No! That's extraordinary!' They looked at each other in amazed admiration. 'Do tell us about it.'

'I opened the refrigerator.'

A gasp of anticipation.

'And took out a bottle of milk.'

Hysterical laughter.

Etc. Etc.

After a while the actor began to time these mundane statements as if they were pearls of wisdom. He got used to people reacting as if everything he said was witty and brilliant and he learned how to behave the way that witty and brilliant people behave. When he next rehearsed the scene in the play I asked him to imagine a crowd of admirers around him whenever he spoke. He didn't have to create witty dialogue because Noël Coward had done that for him, but the improvisation had taught him how to deliver the lines with confidence. It worked. It was brilliant. He was brilliant.

The Cherry Orchard by Anton Chekhov

The relationships between the masters and the servants in *The Cherry Orchard* are quite complicated because all the characters have known each other for a long time. In order to help the actors to understand the complex status structure within the play, the actors playing the servants can be treated like servants themselves. For instance, the actors playing the employers could get the actors playing servants to set up the rehearsal room at the beginning of each day and tidy it up at the end. However, the 'servants' wouldn't have to do this unless they were told to by the 'employers'.

It sounds like an easy exercise and, to start with, the actors playing high-status characters may enjoy being bossy with the actors playing low-status characters. But after a few days the 'servants' will became a bit cheesed-off with being given orders and they may choose not to turn up for rehearsals until the last minute in order to avoid having to do the work. They may also become rather stroppy and unhelpful. When this happens the 'employers' will have to find a way of dealing with the situation and as a result they will begin to understand the problems of having servants. They know the room has to be set up, but the 'employers' aren't allowed to do it themselves so they have to find a way to negotiate with the 'servants'. They may have to charm them, or be extremely authoritarian with them, but however they do it, this exercise will help them discover exactly what is required to get servants to work for them while keeping a reasonably harmonious atmosphere in the room. The actors playing servants may discover that if they are too easy to handle, they will be given all the work! In fact, the masters and mistresses of the house may became a little frightened of any of the stroppy 'servants' and treat them with greater respect and give them more responsible jobs.

Drama Triangle

There's an interesting exercise that is adapted from an exploration of family relationships in a book by Thomas A. Harris called *I'm OK, You're OK*, where he describes a triangular relationship in which one person is the persecutor, another is the victim and the third is the rescuer. When I use this as an exercise I put people into groups of three and ask them to give themselves roles in a family situation. There are many variations of this: father/mother/child; brother/sister/mother; grandmother/

son/granddaughter, etc. It works with any of these and many more, but as an example I will use the relationship between a father, a mother and a son.

Let's say they decide that the father is the oppressor, the son is the victim and the mother is the rescuer. I ask them to improvise a scene and off they go. The father bullies the son, the son feels miserable, and the mother tries to save the situation. However, several things can happen. It's usually quite simple for the father to oppress the son, but sometimes the son will find it hard to be victimised. He will want to fight back, but he's not allowed to because he has to be a victim. The mother will step in and try to make the son feel better, but she may then turn to the father and start having a go at him. But of course she's not allowed to do this because she will then be oppressing the father and she is supposed to be the rescuer. These are three very distinctive roles.

As an example of the drama triangle I often cite *Fawlty Towers*. In this celebrated sitcom, Basil Fawlty always oppresses the waiter, Manuel. Manuel never fights back because he is a born victim. He takes his punishment and feels bad. But Polly, the maid, often steps in to save the situation. She doesn't oppress Basil, she reasons with him and tries to rescue Manuel and cheer him up.

Back to the family group. Having got everyone to understand the nature of the drama triangle, I ask them to give it another go and it usually works out fine.

Then I ask the actors to stay as the same characters, but to swap the roles around. The mother may become the oppressor, the father becomes the victim and the son is the rescuer. It's an interesting variation. As the actors do this next improvisation they begin to understand the differences in family life.

I then ask the actors to do the third version. The son oppresses the mother, the mother is the victim and the father is the rescuer. It still works! In fact, it can work in any combination, in any situation.

But what makes it interesting for the actors is that, as *people*, they tend to fit into one of these three roles. In a discussion afterwards some of them will say it was easier to be the persecutor, some will say they liked being the rescuer and others felt more at home as the victim. Similarly, each person will have found it particularly hard to be either of the other roles. They are amazed when several people say they found it easy to be the persecutor. Some are gobsmacked that others liked to be the victim or the rescuer. But what they all start to understand is that they have to learn how to take on relationship roles that are unfamiliar to them.

This is particularly useful in rehearsals if an actor is playing a character who is a persecutor, for instance, and they are by nature a victim or a rescuer. By doing this exercise, it helps the actors understand how to step outside their comfort zone and learn, in this case, how to persecute.

Look Back in Anger by John Osborne

Look Back in Anger explores the disintegrating relationship between Jimmy Porter and his wife Alison, who live in a one-room attic apartment. Jimmy's best friend Cliff lives in a bedroom across the hall and often drops in to visit. The character of Jimmy Porter has famously become known as 'the angry young man' because throughout the play he has continual tirades against middle-class England. Alison is from a middle-class background and, consequently, she is often the butt of his anger. Cliff hates to see them argue and tries to step in to stop it. This is a classic drama triangle with persecutor (Jimmy), victim (Alison) and rescuer (Cliff).

In character, the three actors could improvise a scene where they take on undiluted versions of these roles. Jimmy persecuting one hundred per cent, Alison totally suffering as the victim, and Cliff trying to rescue the situation without upsetting anyone. It will seem just like a scene from the play. Then, still in character, but shifting around their roles they could try another improvisation. Alison could become the persecutor, Cliff the victim and Jimmy the rescuer. They could then do a third improvisation with Cliff as the persecutor, Jimmy as the victim and Alison the rescuer. The results will be fascinating, but they will also uncover a deeper complexity in the relationship between the three characters. Of course, Jimmy persecutes Alison throughout the play, but there is more to their relationship than that, as is revealed in the final scene where they play a game in which Jimmy pretends to be a bear and Alison pretends to be a squirrel. During the play, Cliff may rescue the situation as much as he can, but he is a friend of Jimmy's and, as such, he would sometimes have to match Jimmy's strength face to face. Of course Alison is Jimmy's victim, but she also has a rescuing side to her personality.

After experimenting with these variations, the actors will be able to understand how the complex relationships between these three people could possibly work and they will be able to create a more subtle and intricate version of this complicated triangle as the rehearsals progress. Nothing is as simple as it may appear.

Further Background Improvisations

It is impossible to be specific about any further background improvisations that you could use because every production will present different problems and/or opportunities. But I think it will be useful if I describe, in some detail, the background improvisations I used when I was working on one particular play to give you an idea of the type of work which is beneficial. As always, the purpose of the improvisations is to explore and clarify certain aspects of the play by combining prior knowledge and research with the imaginations of the actors involved.

Someone Who'll Watch Over Me by Frank McGuinness is inspired by the hostage crisis in the late 1980s in which John

McCarthy and Brian Keenan, amongst others, were taken hostage in Beirut and held captive for a number of years. The whole action of the play takes place in a cell and the only characters are three hostages chained to a wall. It's a fascinating exploration of fear, loneliness and boredom, as well as an insight into relationships and the human condition.

As part of our research, the actors and I watched documentaries about this crisis and read several books, but we felt that we needed some deeper understanding of the political background of the incident. What was it like for the government who had to deal with this situation? How did the hostage-takers feel about it and why did they do it? What were the hostage-takers like and how would that impact on the three prisoners?

Although there are only three characters in the play, I was working with a number of student actors, who took it in turns to play the different scenes, so I had quite a lot of actors to work with.

I set up the following series of exploratory exercises and improvisations:

Opposing Opinions

To try to get some sort of balanced view of opposing opinions, I divided the group into two halves and set up an improvisation about whether the earth was round or flat. I told them that this should take place at a time in history when the accepted belief was that the world was flat. Four people who believed that the world was round were to give a lecture about why they had that opinion. The rest of the group were allowed to heckle and argue as much as they liked.

Although the lecture was reasonably calm when it started, it soon became very heated, with people screaming their opinions and hurling abuse at those who didn't think the way they did. When we discussed the improvisation afterwards, everyone agreed that it was extremely annoying when other people didn't think the way they did. In fact, it made them angry. Different opinions can lead to violent reactions, and violence can lead to war, as people fight for their beliefs.

Political Problems

The next two improvisations were a continuation of this theme. Firstly, I asked half the group to improvise while the other half watched.

The scenario was a meeting of high-ranking politicians and advisors. I gave each of the improvisers a particular character to play as follows:

- The President of the United States
- A presidential aide who wants the President to stay in power
- A military advisor
- A high-ranking Christian leader
- A businessman who sells armaments to the Middle East
- A liberal humanitarian
- A representative of the Lebanese government
- An American counterintelligence officer (spy)

I then told them that three American hostages had been taken in Beirut and that the President had called a meeting to discuss how to handle the problem.

The results were interesting. Military retaliation was discussed. Negotiation and a diplomatic resolution became part of the improvisation. Methods of rescue were planned. It was all rather heated and lively. After the improvisation, the overriding feeling from the actors was that the taking of hostages had created a complex problem that had no easy solutions and it would have taken a lot more discussion before there was any sort of resolution.

I then asked the other half of the group to set up a similar improvisation where they were high-ranking Arab leaders holding a meeting. I gave them characters as follows:

- The President (a Christian)
- The Prime Minister (a Muslim)
- A military advisor
- A person who negotiates with the West
- The American ambassador
- A Muslim fundamentalist
- A Muslim counterintelligence officer (spy)

I told them that three American hostages had been taken by a group of terrorists from their own country and the meeting had been called to discuss the problem and how to handle it.

Interestingly enough, the results were much the same as the previous improvisation: a very heated discussion with a number of conflicting solutions and a strong feeling that the problem was extremely complicated and couldn't be solved overnight.

Different groups could easily come up with other conclusions, but the important thing with an improvisation like that is to try not to prejudge the outcome. Let the improvisation go wherever it may go, let the findings be whatever they may be. See what happens, discuss the results and learn without prejudice.

⚡ The Hostage-takers

Although neither the guards nor the hostage-takers appear in the play, I was determined to give the actors some sort of insight into who these people were and why they did what they did. After all, the hostage-takers must have been a strong background presence for the hostages as they were manhandled and moved around. At any time, one of the guards could burst into the cell and take a hostage out to be shot. Obviously we had done a lot of research, so we had some idea of the type of people who performed these acts of terrorism, but the actors needed to have some practical experience of who might be lurking outside their cell while the hostages were being held captive. The best way to do that was to set up an improvisation to explore what it might be like to be a terrorist.

First of all, I asked all the actors to become hostage-takers and to imagine that they had just taken three people hostage on the streets of Beirut that morning. I asked them to stand outside the door of the rehearsal room and then burst into the room as if they had just locked the hostages up and were returning to their headquarters.

⚡ The Hostage-takers' Characters

The improvisation was reasonably satisfactory, but I felt that they had all become stereotypically 'mad' terrorists. To me that wasn't very helpful. All groups, even groups of terrorists, are composed of individuals with different backgrounds and objectives. So I gave each person a character as follows:

- An organiser
- A vicious bastard
- A fifteen-year-old
- A father with two young kids
- The son of a rich family
- An armament obsessive
- A military tactician
- A university student studying to be a doctor
- Two close friends
- Someone who got kicked in the face during the hostage-taking

Then they tried the improvisation again and it seemed to make much more sense. There were varied reactions, conflict and doubt, but there was still something lacking. There was no adrenalin. No sense of victory.

⚡ The Celebration of Success

I suggested that the actors should forget about being hostage-takers for a bit and do something entirely different. I asked them to be football supporters in a pub watching their national team play a very important match on television. I told them that the score was one-all and it was the last few minutes of the game. The improvisation started and I talked them through some exciting action on the screen. They were on the edge of their seats as the tension built. Bursts of optimism followed by groans of disappointment. I counted down the last three or four minutes of the game and then, just as the whistle was about to blow, I told them that their team had scored the winning goal. They erupted with excitement. I let the improvisation continue for at least ten minutes in order to see what they would do.

Afterwards we discussed what had happened and how they had behaved. We identified some familiar things that they had done and that football supporters often do when their team has won. For instance, there was a strong sense of patriotism. People paraded an imaginary flag in their team's colours and sung patriotic songs. They also sung songs of victory ('We are the Champions!') and punched the air. They danced up and down and flung their arms around each other, grinning wildly into each other's faces. They described exciting bits of action to each other. Their eyes glinted with hero-worship as they mentioned individual players and yet they used their nicknames as if they were best mates. They shouted and gave each other high-fives. Sometimes they jumped on each other, and sometimes they just sat around looking shellshocked and amazed.

In discussion afterwards, I suggested that all this activity could be caused by a build-up of tension and the subsequent release of adrenalin, and that could be how the hostage-takers might have felt after a successful mission. They must have been just as nervous, excited and anxious as football supporters. After all, they had no idea what would happen. Someone could have been injured. The hostages could have had guns. It could all have gone wrong. So there would have been a similar build-up of adrenalin ready to be released the moment they were assured of success.

The Group of Individuals

I suggested that the actors try the original improvisation again, taking note of all the various ways that the football supporters had behaved and applying them to the hostage-takers' celebration.

The result was very informative. The hostage-takers were no longer stereotypical clichés but instead they became a mixed bunch of individuals who reacted to their mission in a number of different ways. In short, they became human beings that the actors could believe in and have some sort of feeling for. The funny thing is that the hostages that they were supposed to have taken during the improvisation didn't have individual personalities at all. As hostage-takers, the actors talked about the hostages as if they were all the same. The hostages had now become the stereotypical clichés! We decided that, whichever side people are on, they don't view the opposition as individuals; they see them, en masse, as 'the enemy'.

The Hostage-takers' Families

Next, I wanted to give these hostage-takers more of a life outside terrorism, so I asked the actors to get into groups of five. One person was to be the same hostage-taker that they had been in the previous improvisation, and the other four had to take on the roles of that character's family. They could be the hostage-taker's parents, or brothers and sisters, or children or grandparents, uncles or aunts. Or any combination. It was up to them.

The scenario for the improvisation was to be the hostage-taker going back to his family for a meal after the celebration of the previous improvisation. Most of the family should know that the hostage-taker had been involved in a mission earlier that day and probably knew what the mission involved. Some should approve and think he was a hero, while the others should disapprove, either for political reasons or because they were worried for his safety. I asked each group to give themselves roles, make these decisions, and then start the improvisation.

There were some interesting and varied versions of this improvisation. Some of the families were lively, either with excitement or relief; while others were more philosophical or political. Some families wanted to know exactly what had happened and others wanted to get on with the meal.

These variations in family life and the different reactions of relatives seemed to reinforce the notion that there was no archetypal hostage-taker. Everyone is different.

⚡ The Guards

By now, the actors had created several quite different hostage-takers with complex characters and lives, so the next thing I wanted to do was to give the actors a sense of what the hostages might have felt about the guards and what the guards might have felt about the hostages. I asked everyone to stay in the same groups, but this time the actors who had been family members in the previous improvisation would now become the hostages themselves. I asked each group to set up an area of the room as if it were a cell. I explained that it was the day after the mission and the hostage-takers were taking their turn to guard the hostages. The hostages couldn't speak Arabic but the hostage-takers had a smattering of English. We blindfolded the hostages and left them alone in their 'cells' to establish some feeling of what it might have felt like, while I took the guards (hostage-takers) into the corridor to explain what I wanted them to do.

Once outside the room we discussed how the guards might feel about the hostages. The actors had created a range of emotions and opinions during the previous improvisations, from hatred of the 'ungodly Western bastards' to a humane sympathy for their plight. Someone suggested that the guards could be scared of the hostages and someone else felt that they wouldn't know how to deal with them. After leaving the hostages in their cells for about five minutes, I explained to the guards that it was their first day on guard duty and they were to take the hostages some food and see how they were getting on.

Again, the improvisations were quite varied. When the guards arrived, some of the hostages had already started to talk to each other, while others were still sitting silently, waiting for something to happen. All the hostages were frightened of the guards and very uncooperative. Some were quite aggressive. One guard didn't say anything at all when he entered the cell; he just shoved the hostages with his foot and tried to put plates of food in their hands. Don't forget that the hostages had blindfolds on, so they had no idea what was going on. They didn't even know that the guard had a plate of food, because, naturally, we didn't have any props, so they were very confused. Another guard was quite authoritative. In broken English he ordered people to stand up, move to different places in the cell and then sit down again. He was quite aggressive as he shoved them around. A third guard tried to talk to his hostages as he spoonfed them. He told them they must eat, and that the food was good for them and it would keep them healthy. In another cell the hostages were quite aggressive themselves and fired questions at the guard, but the guard couldn't understand what they were saying.

All these seemed to be acceptable variations of how it might have been. Afterwards, everyone said that the strongest feeling was one of confusion and uncertainty. Neither the hostages nor the guards knew what was expected of them in a situation like that and they just didn't know what to do or how to behave.

⚡ The Friendly Guard

Having read Brian Keenan's book, *An Evil Cradling*, about his experiences as a hostage, we knew that some of the guards became quite friendly, so I decided to take these improvisations a step further. I told everyone it was about a month later and then I called the guards out of the room and left the hostages in their cells again, still blindfolded. This time I told the guards that they should try to make friends with the hostages. They could offer them cigarettes and get to know their names. They could try to discuss each other's families. They could do or say anything that they thought the guards might do to establish some sort of empathy and friendship.

Once again, the improvisations were varied. The hostages were extremely wary when these expressions of friendship were offered. They thought it might be a trick. They hated the guards anyway, because they had been kidnapped by them so it was very hard to view them as friends. The guards really had to work at it. But gradually the ice melted and an uncertain trust evolved.

We felt that this 'uncertain trust' of the guards was how the hostages must have felt for a large part of the play itself. Although they knew the guards were their enemy and that some were nicer than others, there was a feeling that things could change at any moment.

I decided to explore that.

⚡ The Unexpected

For the next improvisation I told everyone that it was four months later. The same people were in the same cells and they were being guarded by the same guard. However, by now, this guard had become quite friendly and was someone the hostages felt at ease with. Before the improvisation started I told them that I myself would be taking a role in this improvisation, but I didn't tell them what it would be.

After a brief chat outside the room, I send the guards back to the cells to talk with the hostages in a friendly fashion. It was interesting. The guards and their hostages talked about the news on the radio, or life back in the hostages' country. The guards talked about their families and so did the hostages, but everyone was rather tentative around political subjects. The conversations were mostly about things that people had in common rather than their differences.

After about ten minutes I shouted out, 'Guards. Come to my office!' – and I left the room. The guards came out into the corridor and I said, 'We have to show the Western governments that we mean business. I want each of you to take a hostage from a cell and bring them out here to be shot!'

The guards were shocked. Their jaws dropped and they looked extremely pale as they went back into the room. They became monosyllabic and aggressive as they manhandled the hostages and shouted at them. 'Get up!' 'Be quiet!' 'Come with me!' The hostages were terrified. They were still blindfolded and they had no idea what was going on. The guards each grabbed a hostage and pushed them out of the room. I indicated that they should line them up against the wall. Then I bashed a long piece of wood against the floor to make a sound like a rifle shot. Then I did it three more times. Everyone in the corridor was silent and shocked. We stayed there for about five more minutes. When we went back in the room some of the hostages were crying. Some were huddled in silent groups. Some were whispering fearfully to each other.

I stopped the improvisation and told everyone to take their blindfolds off.

Discussion

There was a long discussion afterwards. Hostages actually had been shot during the hostage crises which had inspired *Someone Who'll Watch Over Me*, and the horror of that was brought home to us very clearly. The hostages left in the cell had been shocked and scared. For a start they couldn't understand why the guards had suddenly become so aggressive, when a few minutes earlier they had been chatting about each other's lives and families. And, because they were blindfolded, they weren't even sure who had been taken out. They definitely didn't know what was going to happen next and they were very frightened. These improvisations had been going on for over an hour and everyone was seriously involved and committed.

These were very useful improvisations for the hostages to get an understanding of the pressures and fears that their characters would be going through, but perhaps the most revealing incident was when the guards had to go to select a hostage to be taken out and killed. We discovered that their aggression was the product of their own feelings of confusion. One minute they had been talking with the hostages in a relaxed and friendly fashion and the next they were selecting someone to be shot. We discovered that their aggression was a way of distancing themselves from their inhumane actions. It felt wrong for the guards to remain friendly when they had to be involved in an execution, so they did the opposite. They barked out orders and pushed and shoved. When I asked them what had influenced their choice of hostage they all agreed that they had chosen the person that they had bonded with least. The hostage that had been the quietest or the hostage that had been the least friendly. All the guards said they felt like shit as they had taken someone out to be shot.

Well, yes.

I've gone into a lot of detail about background improvisations for *Someone Who'll Watch Over Me* in order to explain how each improvisation can lead to the next as more and more discoveries are made. It is impossible to prescribe a set of background improvisations that would suit each and every play. I would suggest that the director and the cast decide what the actors need to experience in order to fully understand their characters' internal emotions. These things don't have to be part of the actual plot of the play, but they are things that will have affected the inner life of the characters. Then, as each improvisation reveals a better understanding, the director and the cast can discuss what to explore in the next improvisation until the actors have built a complex network of emotional experiences to carry with them into future rehearsals.

4

Preparing a Character

Years ago there was a documentary on television called *The Epic That Never Was*. It was about the making of a film version of Robert Graves's book *I, Claudius*, and it was to be produced by Alexander Korda, directed by Josef von Sternberg and starring Charles Laughton as Claudius. The film never got finished, partially because Merle Oberon (playing Messalina) had a bad car accident, but also because there were a lot of artistic problems between the actor, director and producer, who were all larger-than-life personalities. The documentary suggests that Merle Oberon's car crash was an excuse to pull the plug on a doomed project.

What is fascinating to watch in the thirty minutes of material that still exists from the original shooting is the struggle that Charles Laughton appears to have in creating the character of Claudius. There are quite a few outtakes, including moments when Laughton abandons a scene and, with the camera still rolling, complains that he can't get the character right.

I have a vivid memory of becoming engrossed in Charles Laughton's intense struggle as I watched the documentary. He had already won an Oscar for his performance in *The Private Life of Henry VIII* and the previous year he had been nominated for his portrayal of Captain Bligh in *Mutiny on the Bounty*, so he had a lot to feel confident about; but the outtakes show him in a state of high anxiety about the smallest details of the part. It was a revelation to realise that the artistic struggle continues throughout life, no matter how much success a person has had in the past.

The interesting thing watching the scenes that do exist is that Charles Laughton seemed to have developed a very clear version of a very complex character, but the outtakes also show that he was never really satisfied. That is until shortly before filming was abandoned for good, when he joyfully declared that he had found the character.

He said that Claudius was Henry VIII!

This is very revealing to me because, obviously, Laughton's Claudius is nothing like his Henry VIII in the scenes we see. Laughton's Henry was a larger-than-life, arrogant, lascivious, gluttonous monster, whereas his version of Claudius is a shambling, stammering halfwit (I'm being a bit unfair, but that's how he comes across).

So what's going on here? How could he mean that both characters were alike?

Well, I think it's all about the process of character creation. When an actor first starts to take on a role, he or she is dealing with an alien, someone whose persona is a mystery to them. The character's actions may be clear, but their motivations are yet to be discovered, their personality is in the script, but it seems to be hidden; and in the early stages of rehearsal it's impossible to understand the complexity of that personality. The character's history exists but, like the pieces of a jigsaw, it needs constructing to get the complete picture.

When an actor first tries to 'become' a character it's like putting on a new pair of shoes which sort of fit, but are uncomfortable and awkward to move about in. The actor needs to 'break in' a new character until it's comfortable to wear, just like a pair of new shoes, and that takes time. Poor Charles Laughton, he had to go through that agonising and insecure period of creation with the cameras rolling and the superstar director marching about unsympathetically and impatiently. No wonder he was stressed.

And when he happily declared that Claudius was Henry VIII, what he must actually have felt was that he had become as comfortable in the role of Claudius as he had been when he played Henry VIII. And when an actor is comfortable in a role, it doesn't feel like acting at all. It feels like 'being'.

And that, for Charles Laughton, was the similarity between the two dissimilar roles. In both cases a part of him felt that he had become the character. And when that happens, everything starts to feel better.

IMPROVISING IN THE EARLY STAGES OF REHEARSAL IS A fabulous opportunity to 'break in' a character without any pressures. Not only is the actor free from the microscopic gaze of an audience, he or she doesn't even have the pressure of making someone else's words come alive. They don't have any anxiety about the tempo of a scene, and their characters don't have to stumble through difficult emotional relationships with the embryonic characterisations of other struggling actors. As one improvisation leads to another, the actors can just 'be' their characters and find out what happens to them in different situations, allowing the complex layers of characterisation to build organically.

The important thing to understand about these early improvisations is that the whole purpose of them is for the actors to discover their characters gradually, bit by bit. There would be no point in creating improvisations if the actors already knew everything about their characters, so it's important that they understand that the sketchy bit of knowledge they have is all they need when they start to improvise. Some of the discoveries they make during early rehearsals may ultimately turn out to be inappropriate, but that doesn't matter. When scientists conduct an experiment and it doesn't turn out the way they expected, it is still regarded as a successful experiment because something has been learned. The same can be said for artistic experiments. The rehearsal room is like a laboratory where the actors can experiment without the threat of failure hanging over them. There can be no failure, because an exploration into new territories always brings unexpected discoveries. Some actors like to keep experimenting with an idea for weeks, trying to make it work. Why not? That's what rehearsals are for.

Where to Start?

There are no hard and fast rules about what will work in the early stages of rehearsal, but in order to give each actor some sort of characterisation to improvise with, there are a number of different exercises which explore physical and vocal qualities. This way the actor can let their body become a physical structure to be filled with subtle layers of characterisation. They don't have to be bothered about how their character feels, they can just concentrate on how their character moves and speaks.

Well, you've got to start somewhere.

I usually try three different physical explorations to see what will 'fit' for each actor as he or she starts to build a character. Not only do different things work for different actors, but different things work for different plays and in the creation of different characters at different times. The actors never know what will be the best way for them to explore a character until they try things out, but the great thing about these explorations is that they take advantage of the actors' greatest creative tool: their imagination!

Physical Exploration 1 – Centres

Many professional actors are familiar with Michael Chekhov's concept of a 'centre' for their character, but if you are working with actors who aren't, then it is worth running through a brief exploration of the idea with them. To my way of thinking, the 'centre' of a character is the point of focus for their physical movement through the world. The actual point of balance for a human being is somewhere around their navel. Apparently when astronauts are in a zero-gravity situation, they cannot shift their physical centre without touching something solid to push off from. They can flail around as much as they like with their arms and legs and even get their bodies to turn, but they can't move from one place to another without pulling or pushing against the walls. That's where the neutral physical centre is. The point in the body around which everything else is balanced.

Exploring Centres

First of all, ask the actors to move around the room exploring that balanced – as it were, 'centred' – centre. Then ask them to move their physical attention – their centre – to a point on their chest, or their shoulders, to see how it affects the way they move. They can try their centre being in their knees or their feet or even the tips of their noses. Every new imagined physical centre will adjust the way that a person moves.

The physical centre can also be outside the body. It could be a point ten centimetres behind the shoulders, or twenty centimetres above the head. It could also be a movable point, orbiting the brain, or the stomach. Ask them to try these suggestions out and they will soon get the idea.

Then ask them to experiment with different centres for the particular character they are working on. First, you can ask them to try the obvious – Hamlet's centre in his brain, for instance, or Romeo's in his heart – and when they feel comfortable with that, suggest that they try the less obvious – Hamlet could try a centre in his shoulders, Romeo could try one in his groin. They should discover for themselves which imagined physical centre seems to fit: the centre that makes them feel that they are becoming the character they are in the process of creating.

With each exploration of a new centre, ask the actors to try strolling around. And then try running. They should try sitting on a chair and standing up. Opening the door, leaving the room and then coming back in again, lazing in the sun or sheltering from the rain. Experimenting with various simple activities and tempos to see what happens. Having tried several different centres they can then decide which seems to be the most useful.

Once everyone is satisfied that they have something to work with, get them to snap out of character and walk around as themselves. (I usually do this with a clap of the hands to give them a clear moment of change.) Then almost immediately snap them back into character again. Repeat this several times until they begin to discover a 'key' to their character's centre. Something that is different from themselves: a way they hold their shoulders, a tilt of the head; a physical change which immediately makes them feel like someone else. This is not a deep understanding of the inner workings of a character's mind. It's a trick, if you like, to give them a starting point in the creation of a character. The first daubs of paint on a canvas that will help to create a basic structure for the painting.

Physical Exploration 2 – Energy States

Different people have different internal rhythms, or energy states. Of course, there are all sorts of different internal rhythms, but, by adapting an exercise I learned from John Wright, I have tried to isolate an 'energy scale' from one to ten starting with 'Catatonic' (no energy) and ending with 'Rigid' (so much energy that the body short-circuits as it becomes massively tense).

The interesting thing about energy states is that actors very rarely move from their own personal energy state when they create a character. They will alter the way they walk to suit a character, or they will adjust their weight, their centre, their voice and/or their accent, but a 'Laid-back' actor usually finds a 'Laid-back' energy for their character. An 'Ecstatic' actor plays every character with an 'Ecstatic' energy.

Exploring Energy States

Here are the energy states that I use:

- *Catatonic*   No energy, immovable
- *Lethargic*   Minimal energy
- *Laid-back*   Relaxed energy
- *Efficient*   Economic energy
- *Neutral*   Balanced energy
- *Alert*   Controlled energy
- *Ecstatic*   Excited energy
- *Passionate*   Fanatical energy
- *Hysterical*   Frenzied energy
- *Rigid*   Massive energy, immovable

To introduce a group of actors to these different energy states, work through them one by one to give everyone a chance to experience them for themselves.

Catatonic

Ask the actors to explore the idea of having no energy whatsoever. Really explore it. At first they will probably stop walking and let their shoulders droop, but then they will gradually get the idea that if they don't have any energy at all, they won't even be able to hold their bodies up and they will sink to the floor and lie there. If they have no energy, they can't move at all, so, unless they are playing a corpse, this is unusable for an actor. Explain that it's only there as a starting point on the scale. Zero, if you like.

Lethargic

Next, ask them to explore the idea of having minimal energy. They should use as little energy as possible to perform any task. Unless they need to do something, they shouldn't move. They should just stand where they are. Even getting a chair to sit on is using too much energy. However, if they want to get from one part of the room to another, they should do it slowly and directly, so there is no waste of energy. Ask them to explore this on their own and then suggest that they have minimal conversations with other people in this lethargic state. Again, they should be as frugal as possible in their choice of words and the use of their voices. Everything – walking, talking, thinking – should be accomplished using the least amount of energy possible.

Laid-back

As with all of these, the name of the energy state, combined with the description, is a good starting point for the actors. For this state, ask them to move around in that relaxed, easy manner that is usually associated with Californians. No hassle. Everything is effortless. A bit drifty. The interesting thing about this energy state is that plenty can be accomplished, but nothing is hurried or anxiety-ridden. As before, ask them to have conversations in this energy state to see how it affects the way they talk. Then ask them to plan an evening out. Making plans should be no problem. Life is stress-free. Relaxed. Laid-back.

Efficient

This is economic energy. Exactly the right amount of energy to accomplish any task. If one needs to get from one place to another, one takes a pause, considers the pros and cons of the journey and makes a decision that will balance the time spent taking the journey with the energy expended during the journey, in order to optimise an efficient outcome. As before, first ask the actors to try this out on their own and then suggest they have conversations with other people. Everything – sitting, standing, moving, talking, thinking – is accomplished economically and precisely.

At this point it's useful to get a third of the actors to be 'Lethargic', a third to be 'Laid-back', and a third to be 'Efficient', and then ask them to intermingle and have conversations with each other. This way they will see how these changes are really just variations of the way that people actually behave.

Neutral

This is a balanced state. Ask the actors to try to find a way of being that is in harmony with their surroundings. They should move at the perfect pace to perform any task with equilibrium. Nothing is too fast, and nothing is too slow. The yin and the yang. Everything in accord. The actors should find an agreeably pleasant state of mind that accepts the world as it is. They should 'be on good terms with all persons', as Max Ehrmann says in 'Desiderata'. This is the state of mind that philosophers and spiritual leaders throughout history have tried to achieve. This is the state of mind that most people think is theirs. Ask them to explore this state on their own and then ask them to have conversations with each other. Balanced. Neutral. Harmonious.

Alert

This energy state is controlled – but ready for action. Again, the actors should walk around just trying it out. Ask them to observe everything and be attentive to the world around them. Nothing should pass them by. They should know who is in the room with them and where everyone is. As they move from place to place, every detail of the journey will be clear to them. They should be aware of exactly what the time is and although their energy is under control, they should be mentally prepared for any eventuality. Then ask them to talk to each other within this state. Listening and immediately understanding. Ready for their next move. Alert and in control.

Ecstatic

This energy is excited. There is an enthusiasm about the world. A little too much enthusiasm, perhaps. A state of ecstasy. The light in the eyes. A sense that the truth is marvellous. Ask the actors to explore the way that ecstasy takes them from one part of the room to another as if their path was illuminated by the light of the world. They can't wait to finish their journey across the room. It's as if they are about to discover the truth of life just round the next corner. Then ask them to have conversations with each other. Explore that ecstatic state when someone has a new lover. That assumption that the whole world feels the same sense of adoration. Excited. Ecstatic. Confident and a little too enthusiastic.

Passionate

Taking things a little further, this energy is barely in control. It's about to burst out at any minute. It's like fire as it jumps from place to place without any warning. The actors should find the passion and belief of a creative artist who has found the means of expression. Van Gogh splashing paint about as he captures the life and energy of a flock of crows bursting from a field of oh-so-yellow, oh-so-vibrant wheat. Ask them to move about the room with that passion. Never completely finishing a journey before they start on the next one. Then ask them to talk to each other with that fanatical, almost out-of-control energy. Explore the sense that the world has been created for the glorification of humanity!

Hysterical

Now the energy is out of control, as if the mind is sparking from idea to idea with lightning-like unpredictability and flashes of confusion. Each thought or idea is supplanted by the next before it is properly formed. Each decision is overwhelmed by the next as they burst like fireworks in the brain. The actors should move around the room with no idea why or where they are going or what they want to achieve. Ask them to explore that way of being when the mind can never settle as it creates a wildly confusing storm in their heads. And when they talk with each other they should half-listen, half-talk and half-think of other things. New ideas. That's three halves. Too many halves to make up a whole. Causing hysteria. No control. No possibility for control. No desire for control.

Rigid

By now, the energy is so active that it is unable to find release. It draws into itself and creates a static tension in all directions that is so powerful that movement is impossible. This creates a rigidity in both body and mind that prevents either action or thought. Try it and your eardrums burst.

In fact, like 'Catatonic', this final energy state is impossible for an actor to use. In a real human being it is likely to cause a severe mental and physical breakdown as the body tries to deal with impossible pressure. It is only on the scale to demonstrate the extremes. The outer limits. In fact there are only eight usable energy states. But they are enough to start playing around with.

At this point the actors can each be given one of the energy states from 'Neutral' to 'Hysterical' and allowed to intermingle and interact with each other. This will make the room extremely noisy and things may seem to be completely out of control, but

it's useful because it allows the actors to experiment with these highly active energy states.

Using Energy States

Although people have these different inner rhythms, they have to handle them in some way or another in order to lead their lives. If you look at the characters in the TV sitcom *Friends*, you could say that Phoebe has an 'Hysterical' energy state, but she isn't rushing around all the time shouting and screaming. She deals with it. Yes, her mind is bouncing around from idea to idea but she manages a certain amount of control in order to have reasonable conversations and develop relationships. Ross is reasonably 'Laid-back' but sometimes he has to deal with problems. Monica is rather 'Efficient', but she is still able to have fun, fall in love and get angry. Rachel is, perhaps, 'Neutral' but she can sometimes get quite emotional. Joey is 'Alert' and Chandler is, perhaps, 'Ecstatic', but both of them are sometimes in situations where they have to relax and enjoy themselves. They all have variations of rhythm, but each of their inner clocks tick to a particular beat.

This is not a science, of course, but this breakdown of energy states is a useful tool for an actor during the early stages of character creation. It gives them a point of reference and can be a cornerstone for the construction of a completely new person.

So, as with the centres, ask each person to experiment with different energy states that might suit their character. Allow them to explore these on their own, trying different solo activities as before: running, walking, standing, sitting, etc. When actors get up and 'do' something, they will often discover subtleties that would never have occurred to them through rational decision-making. Experimentation and exploration are the thing.

When the actors feel they have something to work with – an energy state that seems to fit – snap them in and out of character as before with a clap of the hands, so they get used to the 'trick' of using an energy state as a shortcut, a seed from which their character can grow. This appears to discount the concept of taking time to 'get into character', but at this stage the actors will know very little about their characters so, as with the exploration of centres, this should only be seen as a useful tool in the early stages of the work.

Having done these explorations, it will now be possible for the actors to jump from one version of the character to another. They can snap into the character they created using a different centre, and then they can snap out of it. They can snap into the energy-state version of their character and out again as they walk about the room. I usually snap them from themselves to one or the other of the new physical versions of their character and back again several times so they can identify the different physicalities, moods and rhythms that they have created for each physical version of their character.

At this stage, these physical versions of character are not necessarily complementary; in fact, they may even seem to work against each other. But this is rather like reality. Human beings are made of a complex collection of qualities which sometimes seem to be in opposition. For instance, the absent-minded professor, the violent thug who loves children, the exterminating angel. The purpose of this sort of work is to develop intricate and original characters, rather than one-track stereotypes.

Physical Exploration 3 – Animals

The study of animals as a technique for exploring not only the physicality, but the soul of a character, is a complex business and a whole book could be devoted to the subject (and probably has). In order to fully explore this technique, actors will often watch nature programmes on television, or study animals in the zoo, but for an actor in the process of creating a character sketch to use in later improvisations, a much more simple application of the technique can be used.

Exploring Animals

Thanks to television, most people have a reasonably good idea of how the better-known animals look and move. A bear. A lion. A camel. A snake. There are loads of them. Then there are domestic pets like dogs and cats. Hamsters and gerbils. Birds like parrots or budgerigars. Fish like carp or goldfish. Stored inside our brains is a wealth of knowledge about hundreds of living things, and it's that acquired general knowledge of animals that the actors can use as a 'sketch' when they are establishing a simple physical basis for further exploration through improvisation.

As with the previous two exercises, ask everyone to experiment with being two or three different animals that seem to have various qualities of the character they are in the process of creating. It could be a purely physical exploration, as in the case of Laurence Olivier's use of a panther's movements to find an appropriate physicality for Othello, or something more connected to the soul of a character, as in Antony Sher's exploration of the predatory nature of a spider to find the character of Richard III. (Of course, Antony Sher ultimately used both the physicality of a spider as well as the soul, as he describes in his fabulous book *Year of the King*.)

Once the actors have experimented with several different animals – and it should only take a few minutes – they should select the one that seems to be the most useful. Then they should try to 'become' that animal as truthfully as possible, using not only movement but the internal rhythms and mental awareness of their particular choice of animal. Ask them to try to see the world through the eyes of their animal and to think and respond in the way that their animal would think and respond.

When they feel they have found a true way of 'being' their animal, they should gradually transform themselves into a human version of the animal without losing the physical and psychological discoveries they have made. As they change they should become more human in their appearance, but still retain certain physical characteristics and internal rhythms of the animal.

As before, the actors should be given the opportunity to try different animals to see which seems to be the most useful. The one that 'fits'. The animal which makes them feel most 'like' their character.

Putting It Together

Then snap them into changing from themselves into each of the three versions of character they have just explored: centres, energy states and animals. This can be done in a random order until they can transform without thinking. During this process, the actors should begin to discover the version of their character that they feel most comfortable with. The one that they will be able to use as a basis of their character for further exploration through improvisation.

These transformation exercises are to enable actors to experiment with different physical and mental interpretations of character. But they also stop them settling for easy options, or using the tried and tested character transformations that have been successful for them in the past.

Bringing the Character to Life

Having explored centres, energy states and animal characteristics, the actors will have created three different versions of character – sketches if you like – that can now be used to start work on the slow process of giving their characters a 'life'. And the best way to do that is, as always, to allow the actors to use their imagination.

First of all, ask them to lie down on the floor, shut their eyes, and relax, giving them a minute or two to empty their minds. When they have settled, ask them to think about the three versions of their character they have just created and see if they can find a way of combining them into one new person. Can the tiger combine with the passionate energy state and a centre placed in the hips to be all aspects of the same character? By lying down and shutting their eyes, the actors have no distractions from the workings of their minds, and no activities except the free-flow meandering of their imaginations. If they find it hard to combine all three versions, they can combine just two and see if they will fit together. Or failing that, they can pick the one that they were most comfortable with. At this stage, right or wrong doesn't matter, it's merely a question of having a starting point. None of these exercises work all the time; it's the exploration of technique that matters because the truth will be revealed one way or another, through the success or failure of various imaginative exercises.

If none of the exercises have worked for their character on this occasion, the actor can just lie on the floor and concentrate on what he or she has learned about their character from reading the script. (Actually, it's unlikely that none of the exercises will have worked. In my experience, at least one of them will have given each actor something to work with. In fact, the harder task is trying to combine them.)

As they lie on the floor, the actors should let their mental creations feed into their body. They should imagine that their centre is where they discovered it to be and they should imagine the animal characteristics have altered their muscle structure or the workings of their mind, and they should imagine that their energy state is altering their pulse rate and the adrenalin uptake. Give them time to daydream about these things.

At the same time, the actors should start to think about how they imagine their character looks. What is their bone structure or their muscle tone like? Is their skin rough or smooth, pale or tanned? Is it hairy? How do their limbs hang from their bodies? Is their hair a different colour? What is the shape of their nose? Their mouth? Their forehead? They should think about the physical details.

And as they do that, ask them to feel that their character is flowing into their bodies like a liquid. A transforming liquid that flows in through their feet. As it slowly enters them, they should imagine that they are making a physical transformation. At first the feet change into the feet of a new person and then the ankles, followed by the calves. They are slowly becoming someone else. Their knees and their thighs become the character and then their crutch and stomach fills up with the transforming liquid. As the character flows into their internal organs, it starts to affect the way they are. They are becoming someone else. The character flows up through the torso and into the chest and heart. They should start to feel that the beating of their heart is the beating of a new person. Up through their shoulders it flows. Rushing down their arms and into their hands, filling every centimetre with someone else. Their whole body is transforming as the liquid continues to flow. Up through their necks and into their heads. Transforming their faces and infecting their brains so that they are starting to think like a different person. Like their character. Their brains think the thoughts of their character, their hearts beat to a new rhythm and their bodies have a new point of balance.

All this is impossible, of course, but trying to be another person is an impossible task anyway. No actor ever *really* becomes the character they are playing. But they have such tremendous imaginations that they can *believe* they are that character. And their imaginations can work miracles in an exercise like this to find the reality of something that is purely imaginative. They will feel the liquid flow, they will feel the transformation, and they will feel themselves becoming someone else.

Throughout all this, the actors will appear to be doing nothing. Just lying there with their eyes shut. Now it's time for them to slowly come to life. Ask them to open their eyes and view the world as a new person. How does their character see their surroundings and how does their character's brain respond to what they see?

Ask them to get to their feet slowly, but like Frankenstein's Monster, they should examine how each of their limbs works. Their hands are different hands. They move differently. They look at their hands with different eyes. Their arms have a different weight. Their bodies rise from the floor in a different way. Ask them to examine all these changes as they make them. The feeling of their legs and feet as they take the weight of their bodies. The way they balance when they are standing up.

Then ask them to start moving around in this body that is not theirs, with this new brain that affects the way they make decisions. At this stage all thoughts of the original physical transformation can be cast aside. They were bridges to be crossed. Boats to burn. Something new has taken over their creativity. This new character is not an intellectual creation; it is purely imaginative and it plumbs the depths of their intuition.

Exploring the Details

Continuing without a break, ask the actors to explore their character in different solo situations. Suggest that their characters feel relaxed and they are strolling through the park. Then suggest that they are late for an appointment so they can discover how their character might hurry (if indeed they do hurry when they are late for an appointment). Ask them to explore how their characters walk into a room. Do they walk into a familiar room differently from the way they walk into a strange room? Suggest that they find out by trial and error, not making any decisions until they have experimented with alternative versions. What does their character think about when they are waiting for a train, or waiting for a friend, or waiting for a lover? How do they walk in the rain? The things the actors can be asked to explore are endless. How do they behave when they are bored? How do they jump in the air? Keep asking them to try different things and slowly, ounce by ounce, they will build a character in their minds.

Then, as they move around, ask the actors, as their characters, to start describing their actions and vocalising their thoughts quietly to themselves. They should mumble their words as they move around so they can gradually discover how their character talks and the timbre of their character's voice. How does their character articulate their words? Does their character have an accent? How does their character think?

Eventually, ask them to communicate with other people. They should imagine that they don't know each other and then have brief conversations. They can ask someone the time, or ask another person if they know the way to the railway station. These conversations should be very short. Tiny explorations into the way that their characters communicate with strangers. A couple of phrases each and then move on. This is to allow the actors to make mini-experiments. If they feel that the conversation didn't feel right, they can try the same conversation with another person in a different way, to discover something that might feel better. Exploration and experimentation is the path to revelation!

Pooling Discoveries

After this extended piece of creativity, the actors usually need to talk about their discoveries and release their minds from the intensity of such concentrated work. Using their imagination to transform their thoughts and actions is an exhausting business. They will need a bit of a break.

Ask them to share their discoveries with the other actors. They are in the same play together, so any revelation will be valuable to them all. Everyone needs to know about everyone else's character, especially if their characters know each other or meet during the action of the play. If someone says, 'I didn't realise my character was so angry inside', then someone else, who might have a different perspective on that character – even if it's not in the script – would be able to adjust their behaviour to that character accordingly.

There is a lot to learn, and every bit helps.

By now, everyone should have a character to improvise with. I know I spend a long time preparing for the actual improvisations, but without a solid base for their characters, the actors won't be able to make the dangerous explorative leaps into the unknown that create interesting and truthful drama.

The next chapter describes how to use improvisations to build a multilayered character and a lot more will be unearthed. The character decisions or findings so far may well have to be adjusted to accommodate new discoveries. There is a long way to go, but the luggage is packed and the actors are ready for a very revealing journey.

5

Developing a Character

I used to take a lot of photographs. It's a popular pastime for actors because it's creative, time-consuming and you don't need anyone else to do it with you. There's also the possibility of making a bit of extra cash by taking publicity photos for other actors at a very reasonable rate.

I already had an instant point-and-click camera for taking on holiday, but I wanted to get into the sort of photography where you can take arty pictures and possibly hang them on the wall, so I went to get camera advice from a friend of mine who was a professional photographer. Martin was his name, and he was a staff photographer for the *Guardian* so he seemed like a good bet.

He was. He advised me to get a semi-automatic single-lens reflex (SLR). A robust little thing. 'A throwaway camera' he called it because it was cheap. (To him, maybe. To me it was very expensive.) He had several of them. One in his car. One in his briefcase. One on a shelf by the front door. One on his desk. And probably one by his bed and another stuffed up his jumper. He was a journalist, remember, so he had to have a camera ready at all times to snap anything he saw that might be newsworthy.

Soon I was out on the street with my F-stops and my shutter-speeds, clicking away. And then back to Martin's darkroom where he taught me how to develop the film, enlarge the negative, mix the chemicals and print a picture. It was intriguing.

Ah! The darkroom. Yes. This all happened before the proliferation of digital photography. No Photoshop in those days. Just loads of chemicals and multigrade photo paper. What fun.

It wasn't long before I'd built my own darkroom at home and was spending many happy hours taking pictures with my SLR, developing my rolls of film, and printing out eight-by-tens of arty views of London, my friends and things happening in the street. There was a lot to learn. After you've used your camera skills taking a photo, you can adjust the framing and the look of the picture in the darkroom. The original picture, which involved a certain amount of artistic decision-making at the moment it was taken, could then become the springboard for a second round of artistic creativity in the darkroom.

Soon I was taking publicity photos for my friends, production photos for fringe theatre shows, and I even took a couple of cover shots for *Time Out* no less! I was on a roll. There was no end to the attempted development of my photographic skills.

And I didn't stop there. Being an actor I had an interest in filmmaking and being a sixties person I had an interest in comics. Comics that tell stories. Marvel Comics. The Silver Surfer. Steranko. The Fabulous Furry Freak Brothers. Everything from Winsor McCay to Robert Crumb. So one day I was flicking through a book of arty black-and-white photographs by Man Ray or Cartier-Bresson or someone like that when I suddenly thought, 'Wouldn't it be great if these pictures told a story that unfolded as you turned the pages. Like a comic book!'

In that moment I invented the photo-novel in my head. A photographic story that was told picture by picture, but one in which each photograph was a work of art in its own right.

So it wasn't long before I found myself working with a writer called Jonathan Rix. He wrote a script, we sketched out the whole book, page by page, like a massive storyboard, and then we went searching for actors, locations, costumes, props and whatever else was needed.

We picked a three-week slot in everyone's schedules and went out in the streets to take the pictures. It was like making a film. I was still using my little SLR, but I was pushing it to the limits with night shots, action shots, arty shots, slow shutter-speeds, over-exposures and everything I could think of. I think there were about four hundred pictures needed for the book, so, what with retakes and alternative versions, I took about two-and-a-half-thousand pictures in three weeks. My eye was welded to the viewfinder. I was trying to focus my dreams as I slept. It was an exhausting but thrilling three weeks.

And during that time my knowledge of the camera grew and grew.

After the 'shoot', Jonathan and I spent hours in the darkroom, printing out pictures and making mock-ups of some of the pages. It was extremely time-consuming, but my knowledge of darkroom work developed ten-fold.

So although I learned how to use the camera quite quickly and was soon able to take a decent photograph, that wasn't the end. In order to make that photograph into a decent picture and that picture into part of an interesting story, I had to develop my knowledge

by constant experimentation in the darkroom.

And so it is when an actor is creating a character through improvisation. Finding out how the camera worked and taking a photo was rather like the initial exercises in character creation that I outlined in the previous chapter. It was the starting point for all manner of unpredictable developments. In the same way that I developed my photographs, made them into pictures and then used the pictures to create a complex story, I will now describe how to develop a character, make it come alive and then use it to tell the complex story of a play.

In case you're wondering, we got about eight pages of the photo-novel laid out in mock-up form and showed it to several publishers. They were all interested, but no one would commit. Faber and Faber were the most promising. They kept umm-ing and ah-ing for about nine months but eventually even they backed away. They said they didn't know how to market it, and we believed them. Anyway, by that time, Jonathan and I had both moved on to pastures new and we had lost interest in the darkroom. I've still got all the negatives, though. Most of them I've only ever seen on contact sheets. One day... One day.

HAVING GOT THE CHARACTERS WALKING AND TALKING, the next thing is to start to understand how they think and how they behave. Every play is different, of course, so there can be no prescriptive improvisations that will fit all occasions. The director has to be imaginative in deciding what could be the most helpful for the actor. I usually start by working on external influences that might affect the internal development of character. It's often best to let the psychological growth of a character creep up on an actor organically, rather than forcing the actor to make complex psychological decisions too early on. By using improvisation carefully, the actor gradually comes to understand how their character thinks and what drives their character's behaviour.

Clothing

We all like to express ourselves by our choice of clothing, and, in turn, the clothes we wear influence how we behave. I usually wear jeans and a T-shirt to express how relaxed and informal I like to be, so when I dress up in a suit to go to a wedding, I don't really feel like myself. I feel too formal. I'm awkward and uncomfortable, and I start to behave differently. I stand straighter. Upright. Stiff. And in my smart black leather shoes, I place my feet more firmly on the ground. And walk more carefully in case I slip over. I even speak in a more formal manner, rather than mumbling my words and not finishing my sentences properly. Other people, conversely, are hopelessly uncomfortable in jeans. They need to express their personality through finely tailored jackets and trousers.

Women must feel this difference even more strongly when they wear a dress rather than trousers. Or high-heeled shoes rather than trainers. Or if they tie their hair up rather than letting it hang round their face and shoulders. Clothing – and appearance – is a powerful external influence on character.

Getting Dressed

First of all, I ask the actors to take a minute to 'become' their characters by using the information they have learned about physicality and internal rhythm during the previous exercises. Then, as their character, I ask them to imagine that they are getting up in the morning and that they need to decide what clothes they are going to wear for the day. Using the information they have gathered through research, the clothing they choose should be appropriate to the period of the production. As they start this solo improvisation, I tell them that it's an ordinary day, not some special occasion and they are looking for the clothes that they feel most comfortable wearing. As they look through their wardrobe, or their chest of drawers, I ask them to imagine what they see in there. Item by item. Their best clothes, their everyday clothes and the scruffy worn-out clothes that they'll probably only ever wear to dig the garden or paint the walls. I ask them to imagine specialist clothes that their character might have. For instance, they might be the sort of person who sometimes goes hiking, or rides a horse, or exercises in the gym. Then I suggest that they take their imaginary clothes out of their wardrobe, one article at a time. They should look at each piece of clothing and think about it. They should feel the weight and texture of each item of clothing so it starts to become real for them.

As they do this, they should be trying to choose a suitable outfit for an ordinary day. When they have had time to think about these things, I ask them to imagine that they are naked and that they are going to get dressed in the clothes that their character has decided to wear for the day. First they should imagine they are putting on their underwear. What sort of underwear would their character put on, if any? Would they put their socks on first, or their underpants? Would they wear a vest? As they put on each item of clothing I ask them to imagine how it feels on their skin and how it hangs on their bodies. Is it loose-fitting, or is it tight and restricting? How does each item make them feel? Does it affect their behaviour?

Slowly they should continue to dress, putting on the next layer of clothing. Trousers and a shirt. A skirt or a dress. Shoes. Sweaters.

Jackets. As they put on each item of clothing they should continue to imagine how it makes them feel. They can look at themselves in an imaginary mirror to see the changes. Does their character wear jewellery? Would their character wear a tie and cufflinks? A wristwatch? I ask them to add the appropriate accessories. Are there any pockets in their clothing? What is in the pockets? Do they carry heavy objects or light objects around with them? Do they have to fill their pockets with items from a nearby table? Do they put things in a handbag or a backpack? I ask them to imagine how everything they touch feels in their hands. The weight of everything. The colour and the texture.

When they are fully dressed I ask them to try walking around to see how the weight and feel of their imaginary clothing adjusts the way they walk. They should imagine they are going outside. What clothes would they wear to walk down the street? Do they have to put on a coat and a scarf? Or a hat and a cane? Do they wear a sword? Maybe they don't need any additional clothing. Maybe they need to check that they've got their mobile phone. What sort of phone would their character have?

Then, as they are walking down an imaginary street, I ask them to think about how their clothing affects their physicality and self-image. If a number of actors are exploring their characters in this way I ask them to start having minimal conversations with other people in the room as if they were strangers meeting on the street, ignoring the fact that their characters may know each other in the play.

By doing this exercise, the actors discover how external influences affect their characters. By using their imagination they are free from the influence of stage designers or the wardrobe department, so what they are really discovering is how their character would like to dress. By using clothing as a spur to creativity, the actors learn how their character wants other people to see them. It doesn't matter what they actually wear in the production, this exercise is about how the actor thinks their character looks and how they think other people view their character. The imaginary clothing affects both their physicality and their mental state.

Shopping for Clothes

This improvisation is similar to the previous exercise but it allows the character to interact with another character. First of all, each actor must decide where their character would buy their clothes, or how they would obtain them. Then they should decide on some sort of shopping trip that would be suitable for their character, whether it be a trip to Marks and Spencers or a visit to a market stall. A king in a Shakespeare play would perhaps have a selection of new clothes brought to him by his tailor. A character in *Waiting for Godot* by Samuel Beckett may decide to select something to wear from a rubbish tip, or a waste bin in the street. But however they go about it, everybody at one time or another has to acquire new clothing, whether they are interested in what they wear or not. So each actor should decide how his or her character acquires their clothes.

For this improvisation, one of the other actors has to play the part of the sales assistant (or the king's tailor or another tramp in *Waiting for Godot*). They can invent any appropriate character they like to do this, as long as they are truthful to the role. They can be helpful, snooty, obsequious, grumpy or any version of a sales assistant, tailor or tramp that they like, but they must be prepared to discuss the imaginary clothing that the other actor is trying on.

When the improvisation begins, the actor who is shopping for clothes should engage the sales assistant (or the tailor or the other tramp) in a conversation and discuss what sort of clothes they want and why they want them. The sales assistant can give advice and present the shopper with alternatives, describing each item. These items are imaginary, of course. The shopper should then choose a selection and try them on, one by one. The sales assistant can describe how each item makes the shopper look. Particularly pointing out character traits, as in: 'That jacket makes you look very confident' or 'That dress makes you seem extremely open and friendly' or even 'If you wear something like that people will be very cautious around you.' Both people in the improvisation should explore the appearance and the effect of the imaginary clothing. When the shopper feels comfortable, he or she can leave the shop and try 'walking down the street' on their own, as in the previous exercise.

This improvisation presents the actor with alternatives to consider. Their imagination is supported and enhanced by the sales assistant who is coming up with new ideas and new descriptions. Items of clothing that the actor may never have thought about before. The discussion with the sales assistant about the look of the clothes helps the actor discover how their character wants to present themselves to the world.

📖 *Hamlet* by William Shakespeare

During the course of the play we discover that Claudius has killed his brother, the previous king, married the queen and then become the new king himself. Being recently crowned, Claudius has a newfound and unfamiliar status and his choice of clothing could reflect the way he wants to present himself at court. Using the *Shopping for Clothes* improvisation, the actor playing Claudius could be discussing new clothes with his tailor. If the tailor says something like, 'That robe makes you look powerful and dangerous, whereas the one you tried on before gives you the appearance of a party animal', then the actor playing Claudius would start to think about how his character wants other people to view him. Does he want to be seen as powerful, or does he want to be seen as fun-loving? It's an important decision, because both of these character traits are part of Claudius's make-up, and the actor has to decide which version will make his character feel most comfortable when he is surrounded by courtiers. As a result, the improvisation will influence the actor's decision on how he may want to play the part.

⚡ **Letters Home**

This solo improvisation is inspired by a scene in Frank McGuinness's play *Someone Who'll Watch Over Me*, in which each of the hostages speaks aloud the words of a letter they would write home if it were permitted. In the play these letters add to the audience's knowledge of the characters' previous lives, while at the same time they reveal an insight into their individual states of mind at that particular moment.

The idea of a character writing a letter can be used for any character in any play as an exploration of thought and feeling. By actually writing the letter down with pen and paper, the actor is able to focus and clarify his or her character's thoughts and emotions.

Using exercises from the previous chapters, each actor should take a few minutes to 'become' their character, and then, as their character, they should write a letter to someone that their character knows well, telling that person what they are doing and how they are feeling. The actors should be given enough time to allow their imaginations to drift and wander without restraint. I suggest that this improvisation takes place at a point in time before the action of the play, so the actors can discover how their characters feel and what their characters want when they are in a 'normal' state of mind. Neutral. Before the events in the play start to affect both their thoughts and actions.

This exercise can also be used later in the rehearsal process to discover how a character is feeling at a specific point in the play. Hamlet could write a letter to his dead father, perhaps, just before he rushes into his mother's bedroom to confront her with memories of her dead husband. Shylock could write a letter to Tubal just before the court scene. Othello could write to an old friend in Africa when he begins to doubt Desdemona's fidelity. He could even write another letter just before he murders Desdemona. Although Othello is almost mad with jealousy at that point in the play and it would seem unlikely that he would be able to write anything at all, the process of trying to articulate the character's inner thoughts will help the actor develop and understand the complexity of emotion that Othello is experiencing at that time.

Writing a letter gives the actor a focus for their imagination and, if the letter is to someone their character knows well, they will be able to talk about and explore intimate thoughts and feelings. Also, of course, the way the actor makes their character construct sentences – their writing style, their syntax, their vocabulary and so on – is an insight into how their character communicates their thoughts to other people. However, the actors shouldn't try to mimic the language and sentence construction of a period play. It would be very difficult to write in an iambic pentameter, for instance, or use an outmoded vocabulary. Like all the improvisations described in this book, the actor should use the language that the character would use if he or she were alive today.

Helping Each Other

There is a strange resistance amongst actors to allow themselves to be helped by the other actors. 'Don't tell me how to play my part,' people will say. So when I worked with Mark Rylance, he amazed me by asking all the actors to work on each other's parts. He would select a character for the whole cast to discuss and then we would all 'become' that character while the actor playing that part stood to one side to watch. Sometimes, Mark would stand with the actor to discuss what everyone was doing so they could learn from other people's ideas. At other times, Mark would 'become' the character along with everybody else and then, watch out! His imagination knows no bounds. It was all very informative and helpful and everybody learned from everybody else.

The following improvisation uses this idea, but puts it into a slightly different context. It allows the actor to practise his or her role while being exposed to people playing similar characters. In this way, the learning is two-fold. Firstly, the actor has the experience of being in character and, secondly, he or she is surrounded by different versions of the same character.

When I'm setting up improvisations like this, I usually have three or four groups working at the same time, depending on the size of the cast and the size of the rehearsal space. I can then keep an eye on these improvisations by walking from group to group as unobtrusively as possible. As I have said, it is important to avoid any sense of performance when actors are improvising, but it's equally important for the director to see these improvisations so he or she knows what has been discovered by the actors and consequently can make an informed decision about what would be the most helpful thing to do next.

⚡ Like-minded Friends

This group improvisation works best with about four or five actors. One actor in the group will be improvising as his or her character in the play – let's call it the focal character – while the other actors abandon work on their own characters for a while and create characters who are similar to the focal character. They could be a group of friends, they could be work colleagues or they could be people of a similar status. The important thing is that the focal character is surrounded by like-minded people. For instance, if you were working on *Measure for Measure*, Isabella – who is preparing to become a nun – could be chatting with a group of novitiates. Or Blanche DuBois (from *A Streetcar Named Desire* by Tennessee Williams) could be having tea with a group of Southern spinsters. Laertes in *Hamlet* could improvise a scene where he is having a drink with other young men in Paris, or the Prince of Morocco from *The Merchant of Venice* could be with a group of African princes discussing their views of European life.

Before they start the improvisation, the actors should decide where the improvisation is supposed to be taking place and why their characters happen to be getting together to talk. For instance, they could be meeting in a bar to have a drink after work, or they could be in a formal drawing room having tea. They could be hanging out on the street corner watching people go by or they could be sitting in the sun passing the time. The choice of location and the reason for meeting will be informed by the play in question and the character being explored.

Once these things have been decided, the improvisation can get underway. It should continue for at least fifteen minutes to allow the group to become deeply involved in the conversation. At first the actors will talk about things closely related to the play itself or perhaps they will voice stereotypical opinions, but as the improvisation progresses they will start to become more adventurous in their choice of subject matter. They will make unplanned explorations and these will lead to more interesting discoveries.

This improvisation will help the main actor learn about their character through experience, but since they are also surrounded by like-minded people, the actor will be immersed in a 'sea of character' and that will support and intensify their exploration.

Romeo and Juliet by William Shakespeare

As a teenage girl, it would be reasonable to assume that Juliet has other friends who are about the same age and come from a similar background. Teenage girls from all periods of history have probably talked to each other about boys, falling in love and who they would like to marry, and Juliet would be no different. So an improvisation of Juliet chatting with her friends will help the actress understand her character's state of mind at the beginning of the play. She will have the experience of being Juliet before she meets Romeo. Quite different, I imagine, from how Juliet becomes when she falls in love.

In order to highlight other aspects of Juliet's life, Juliet and her friends could also talk about a teenager's relationship with her father, family life, the antagonism of rival gangs, and how the girls feel about the street-fighting that's going on in Verona. These are all things that the actress needs to explore, and by including them in this improvisation she will begin to discover what Juliet feels about different aspects of her life. By sharing thoughts and attitudes with like-minded teenage girls, the actress playing Juliet will develop a greater understanding of her character. Of course, Juliet's friends may not share her opinions, but then Juliet will have to defend her ideas and by doing this, the actress will begin to develop a stronger sense of who Juliet is, and what her attitude is to other important subjects.

⚡ Going Out in Character

A great way to develop and understand the truth of a characterisation is by letting the character interact with the general public
by going out into the real world. For this improvisation, the
actors should wear the sort of clothing that their characters
would actually wear. Within reason, of course. It would be
ridiculous for actors working on *Julius Caesar* to wander up and
down Oxford Street in togas! Or for actresses in *The Importance
of Being Earnest* to wear crinolines, bustles or hooped skirts as
they tried to mingle with shoppers in Harrods. No. The actors
should dress in the sort of clothing that their characters would
wear *if they were alive today*. For instance, Cassius in *Julius Caesar*
was a senator – a politician – so an actor playing Cassius should
wear a suit and tie when he goes out onto the streets because
that is what politicians tend to wear nowadays. An actress
playing Lady Bracknell from *The Importance of Being Earnest*
should try to approximate the sort of clothing that a middle-
aged female member of the aristocracy would wear if she was
shopping in Harrods today. The way people dress affects the way
they are treated by strangers, so it will be very informative for
the actors to see how their character's clothing affects people's
perceptions of them.

Having dressed themselves in the appropriate clothing and taken
the time to 'become' their character, the actors should go out
into the real world and mix with strangers as much as possible.
They should walk like their character, talk like their character,
and when they meet other people, they should express the
feelings and thoughts that their character would have if he or
she were meeting strangers.

This improvisation can, and should, go on for a long time. At
least an hour but preferably longer, so the actors have the
opportunity to talk to shopkeepers, or ask perfect strangers the
way to the station. As time goes by, the actors discover that the
general public will accept them for what they are and they will
start to feel confident in the character they have created.

Just a word of warning: the actors shouldn't let their characters
make any commitments to strangers during this exercise. One of

the people I was working with signed up *as their character* with a charitable organisation who stopped them on the street. On another occasion, an actress gave her phone number to a stranger who wanted to meet her later that week for a drink and without thinking she gave him her real phone number! The actors should avoid this sort of complication by politely extricating themselves from difficult conversations. It's also essential to avoid arguments or fights, even if the character is an argumentative sort of person!

Generally speaking, these complications are easily avoided and the actors return unscathed. They discover that strangers totally believe in the characters and that gives the actors a tremendous confidence in their characterisation. They also learn a lot about the temperament of their characters because they have to react to unexpected incidents without any pre-planning. They have no time to say to themselves, 'How would my character react?' – they just have to be in the moment and go with the flow, and they are often surprised about the way they behave. They will often say that they didn't realise their character was so 'wimpy' or 'flirty' or 'miserable' or whatever. They don't have to go out looking for these things, they just discover them through experience.

Directorial Adjustments

As I watch the improvisations I have described in this chapter, both in the rehearsal room and out on the street, I usually notice various aspects of character that need adjustment. So when the improvisation is over, I hold a group discussion about what has happened and how the actors felt about it. During this discussion I often suggest various changes. Perhaps Juliet needed to be a little more strong-willed, or maybe the actress could have made Juliet seem a little younger. It all depends on what I have observed. I call this 'subliminal direction'. Nudging the actors to make changes rather than giving them instructions. I like to make useful observations which don't quash the actor's creativity and individuality. It's important to give them the freedom to explore, and too many prescriptive demands can be confusing and obstructive. Once the actor is secure in his or her part, they are happy to meet complex and challenging demands – but not at this stage. It's all too delicate because the character is still so new to them. People are always more willing to rise to a challenge when they feel confident and positive about themselves and their work. Give them time. It's still early days.

—

By now, the actors should have a strong sense of who their character is and how he or she thinks. They should also have become accustomed to an altered physicality and an adjusted internal rhythm. They should know how their character likes to dress and they should be able to imagine their surrounding environment. They should understand the social customs of the period and the political climate of the times. In the next chapter I will show how actors can examine the way their character relates to other people and how improvisation can help them build complex and truthful relationships with the other characters in the play.

6

Relationships

Years ago I saw a production of Edward Albee's *Who's Afraid of Virginia Woolf?* The play is about a middle-aged American couple called George and Martha who argue and fight all the time. The action takes place on a particular evening when they have invited a young married couple round for a drink. As the alcohol kicks in, all four characters get amazingly drunk and their inhibitions totally disappear. Everyone's dirty linen is not only washed in public, but hung out to dry. Hatred and frustration, disappointment and disillusion, anger and despair are all expressed in the most violent and graphic of terms, particularly by George and Martha.

As the audience was leaving the theatre I heard someone say, 'I don't know why they didn't split up years ago', and I wanted to scream back, 'They couldn't because they love each other!'

Yes, they love each other. They hate each other. They need each other. They dominate each other. They amuse and entertain each other and they make each other cry. They rescue each other. And they drive each other to drink. They are responsible for each other and yet they want to kill each other. They are trapped in a destructive relationship that is cemented by a desperate need for each other. And if the actors playing the parts don't explore this multilayered, highly complex relationship during rehearsals, then the play can't work. Because who would care? George and Martha would have split up years ago! End of story. No play.

Relationships. It's an endlessly fascinating subject. Two strangers can feel like old friends within a few minutes of meeting each other, while another pair just can't get on the same wavelength no matter how hard, or for how long, they try.

'You must meet Dave. The two of you will get on like a house on fire.' But when you meet Dave, what happens? Nothing. You can't find a common ground. And as for couples, sometimes they're the hardest to fathom. 'What do they see in each other?' people ask, 'They're such an unlikely couple.' 'Yes, but opposites attract... And you never know what goes on behind closed doors' is often the reply.

And it's true. You don't. Couples often like to present a straightforward view of their relationship. Nothing too complicated. They 'don't want people to start talking'. So they may be totally getting on each other's nerves, but everyone else, even their friends, thinks the relationship is harmonious. The perfect couple.

And it's not just an idealistic view that people like to present; sometimes it's quite the opposite. A couple who seem to be in a continual state of conflict can turn out to be each other's best friend. Like George and Martha. Is that what they call a love-hate relationship?

Let's face it, relationships are very complicated affairs, be it business relationships, artistic relationships, domestic, romantic, platonic, sporting or whatever-you-like kind of relationships. They are never straightforward. Talk to anyone who is deeply involved with someone else and they will roll their eyes and say, 'Tell me about it.'

RELATIONSHIPS ARE THE STUFF OF DRAMA. YES, CONFLICT, power, revenge, redemption, love, death, sacrifice and so forth are all contenders, but name me a play that doesn't have at least one interesting relationship in it. If two people have met at least once before, they have a relationship of some sort. A history that will impact on a second meeting. A third meeting. A fifth, tenth, two-hundred-and-tenth meeting. Each time two people meet another dimension is added to their relationship.

There are millions of different plays that contain an unlimited variety of relationships and it would be impossible to describe a generic set of improvisations that would cover all possibilities. But for me it's important for two actors playing characters who have known each other for a while to have the chance to develop a deeper understanding of the relationship between those two characters. I have already mentioned the importance of in-depth relationship discussions in the chapter about preparation, but the actors can now start to *experience* some of their characters' shared history through improvisation. In that way, the actors will create subliminal memories of a shared past.

When I am planning relationship improvisations for a play, there are several avenues of exploration that I look for.

Family Relationships

Perhaps the most complex relationships are within families. Just think of those Christmas celebrations that are fraught with danger as the extended family meets up to spend a day or two together. Talk about multifaceted. So if any characters in a play are members of the same family, I set up improvisations to explore their shared history.

Previous Good Times

Conflict and tension can often be an integral part of a piece of drama. Characters can hate each other or annoy each other or even try to kill each other. But bad relationships often start out well, only turning sour through the passage of time. So if any characters in a play seem to dislike each other, I try to think of an improvisation that will give the actors the chance to explore a time when the characters were on more friendly terms.

Friendships

Friendships are often formed when two people find they just 'click'. They share some sort of empathy that brings them together and creates a long-lasting relationship. So, if two characters in a play seem to have a strong friendship, I set up an improvisation where the actors can experience the moment or moments that their two characters 'clicked' and the relationship began to grow.

Evolving Relationships

The ups and downs of life. The relationships that have gone on for so long that there have been good times and there have been bad times. There have been moments of shared happiness and there have been moments of isolation and grief. If the play focuses on a particularly complex relationship, I set up a series of improvisations which explore various key moments in the development of that relationship.

It will be up to each individual director to create relevant improvisations for the play being rehearsed, but hopefully the following detailed examples will be a helpful guide on how to go about planning useful and informative relationship improvisations.

Family Relationships

I once directed a production of Arthur Miller's *A View from the Bridge*. The play is about a middle-aged Brooklyn couple in the 1950s who are bringing up their teenage niece. Eddie works on the docks, his wife Beatrice looks after the house, and the niece, Catherine, has left school and wants to go to secretarial college. Things start to get complicated when two Sicilian immigrants come to stay in the house and one of them falls in love with Catherine. At the start of the play it appears that the love between Eddie and Beatrice has grown stale, and that Eddie is overprotective of his niece Catherine. But as you delve deeper into the play, it becomes clear that Eddie may have actually fallen in love with his niece. It also becomes clear that Eddie's relationship with his wife is much more complex. She mothers him to a degree, although he is the dominating figure. They have a similar way of teasing each other, yet the teasing can sometimes seem more like an attack. They share dialogue when they are telling a story but get frustrated when their memories are at odds. They shout at each other one minute and they defend one another the next. Their relationship has developed over many years and has become complicated and unique. This is Arthur Miller writing this, and he was a playwright who had a great understanding of the complexity of the human condition.

Then there is the relationship between Catherine and her uncle Eddie. She looks up to him and admires him, but wants to break away from the family and be independent. When she was growing up, Eddie was like a father to Catherine – he protected her, loved her, scolded her and taught her how to deal with life – but now she is an adult he appears to have fallen in love with her. He can't admit that, even to himself. Of course, it's not illegal for Eddie to be in love with Catherine: theirs is not a blood relationship because she is the daughter of his sister-in-law. But, setting aside the fact that he is married, it feels wrong to Eddie because he has raised Catherine like she was his own child.

Of course, his wife Beatrice understands all this but she has an equally complicated relationship with Catherine because, on the one hand, Catherine is the daughter that Beatrice never had, and on the other, she has now become a rival for her husband's attentions. A pseudo-mistress!

Eddie, Beatrice and Catherine are in an extremely complex love triangle, but it's a true love triangle because all three love each other. All three depend on each other and all three want to help and support each other.

If you were to start rehearsing the play – putting it on its feet, as they say – without any preparatory exploration of these relationships, you would continually have to stop a scene and examine it line by line in an attempt to work out what people might be thinking. You would have to refer forwards in the text for clues and you would have to hold long discussions about their relationships. Nothing in Arthur Miller's work is simplistic.

This approach has served directors and actors very well in the past but to my mind there is a problem if you continually stop a scene to talk about it. The actors may learn a lot through discussion, but they need to experience the flow of dialogue to see how their character's inner life fluctuates from moment to moment during the action of the play.

If they were real people, Eddie and Beatrice would have gone through a number of different moods and feelings during their marriage. There would have been times when they were happy; times when they were bored; times when they were passionate; times when they shared their problems; times when they discussed life and how to handle it. And all those experiences would be part of the complex make-up of their relationship. Similarly, Eddie and his niece would have had times of harmony and times of conflict over the years as their lives shifted and changed. The rich tapestry of their relationship would be vibrant and colourful, as would the relationship between Catherine and her aunt. Not only that, these three characters would each have developed relationships with other characters in the play, no matter how tenuous the links may be.

Some of the experiences that the characters might have shared can be improvised by the actors to give a greater understanding of the intricate and complicated nature of their feelings for each other. When the actors eventually start to rehearse the text of the play, this 'knowledge through experience' will affect the way their characters interact.

Towards the end of this chapter I have outlined the relationship improvisations I used when rehearsing A View from the Bridge. Hopefully they will provide a springboard for your imagination when devising improvisations for your own rehearsal process.

⚡ Previous Good Times

When two characters in a play have a difficult, troubled or even disastrous relationship, I like to set up an improvisation where they can experience a time when the relationship was enjoyable, happy and positive. It is particularly valuable when actors are playing characters who loved each other in the past but are now in a state of conflict, because it gives the actors an experiential memory of the time when the relationship was good. Love is a complex web of interweaving experiences and shared moods. Eddie – in *A View from the Bridge* – probably bought Beatrice a bunch of flowers at one time or another. George and Martha – from *Who's Afraid of Virginia Woolf?* – must have been happy in each other's company or they never would have married. Even Lord and Lady Capulet must have held hands under the stars and dreamed of having children, despite the fact that their marriage seems pretty devoid of emotion during the course of *Romeo and Juliet*. All these previous good times must still be part of the relationships years later even if they aren't apparent. If a married couple seem unhappy with each other, they must at least have memories of what they have lost. It's there in their past.

Then there are relationships between parents and children. Did Shylock bounce his daughter Jessica on his knee, sing her silly songs and make her laugh? Most dads do that sort of thing at one time or another. And how about Hamlet and his uncle Claudius, who must have known each other as the young prince was growing up. Perhaps they kicked a ball around the courtyards of Elsinore or went fishing together. Who knows? Maybe Claudius slipped his nephew a fiver, or even explained the birds and the bees to him when he was ten. After all, Hamlet's dad, the king, must have been pretty busy as Hamlet was growing up. Perhaps Hamlet was closer to Claudius than he was to his own father. It could easily be the case. I know that Hamlet's father is a ghost, but in the play he seems to be a pretty distant sort of figure. Massively high-status. Totally self-obsessed. All this could add considerably to Hamlet's problem. Perhaps young Hamlet actually liked Claudius as he was growing up. His favourite uncle. If the actors playing Hamlet and Claudius have discovered a lost intimacy through improvisation, then things become rather interesting.

This relationship between Hamlet and Claudius is pure conjecture, of course. Who's to say that Hamlet didn't hate Claudius all his life? But the point of improvising previous good times is to explore the possibilities. There is nothing in the play to indicate whether Hamlet liked or hated his uncle as he was growing up, so either could be the case. Hate grown out of hate is interesting in itself, but hate that grows out of a close, or even loving, relationship carries a lot of interesting baggage with it. If the actors playing Hamlet and Claudius try to improvise a time when their relationship was positive, they will soon find out if this is workable or not.

There are all sorts of other relationships to explore in *Hamlet* as well as the one between the prince and his uncle. Laertes and Ophelia, for instance. A brother and a sister. Did they play together? Did they argue over toys, or vie for their father's affection when they were growing up? Did Polonius have a favourite child? And what about Juliet and her cousin Tybalt? Did they play happily together or were they constantly at each other's throats? Let the actors improvise their characters when they were children and they will find out for themselves.

These improvisations are intended to bring the characters closer together and help the actors discover an intimacy that has been lost. If it is appropriate, I like to devise romantic or intimate improvisations. These are generally happy times for people. Actors find it easy to improvise conflict and aggression, but it's actually quite hard for them to explore romance, intimacy and closeness. Sometimes I turn the lights down in the rehearsal room to create a romantic mood and give them a sense of privacy. Sometimes I send the actors out for a walk in the park or to Starbucks for a coffee so they can be alone when they make this exploration. When the improvisation has finished the actors can discuss what happened with the director and he or she can make suggestions and adjustments.

Sometimes these 'previous good times' improvisations can involve characters who don't even appear in the play. When Hamlet is given Yorick's skull by a gravedigger, he says:

Alas, poor Yorick! I knew him, Horatio: a fellow of infinite jest, of most excellent fancy: he hath borne me on his back a thousand times; and now, how abhorred in my imagination it is! my gorge rims at it. Here hung those lips that I have kissed I know not how oft. Where be your gibes now? your gambols? your songs? your flashes of merriment, that were wont to set the table on a roar?

At this moment, Hamlet confronts both a symbol of death and a memory of his lost happiness. He is looking at the skull but he is remembering the man who made everyone laugh. Death and happiness are juxtaposed. The problem for the actor is that the sight of the skull is such a potent image that it can overwhelm the memory of happiness.

In order to give the actor playing Hamlet an experiential memory of this happiness, one of the other actors could take on the role of Yorick and they could improvise a scene with Hamlet as a child having fun with the jester. Yorick could carry Hamlet on his back like it's suggested in the script, he could tell Hamlet some jokes and dance about like a clown. So when the actor playing Hamlet rehearses the scene with Yorick's skull, he will have the image of a real face, real fun and a real incident in his mind to remember. This will help to bring the speech to life for the actor.

⚡ Friendships

If two characters are particularly good friends in a play, then it is often valuable to devise an improvisation where they can explore the growth of that friendship. For instance, Rosalind and Celia have a very close friendship in Shakespeare's *As You Like It*, so much so that they both fancy Orlando the minute they see him. They flirt with him and vie for his attention but when Celia realises that Rosalind has actually fallen in love with Orlando, she backs off and supports her friend's romance. (Although she does tease her about it later on in the play.) Their friendship is so strong that when Celia's father, the Duke, banishes Rosalind from the court, Celia decides immediately that she too will leave and go along with Rosalind to the Forest of Arden.

In order to understand this relationship I would set up an improvisation – or a series of improvisations – when the two characters were younger and their friendship was growing. Maybe they would argue with each other, or maybe they would play together, but as they improvised I would ask them to try to discover what it was that made them friends. A shared moment or an unspoken understanding. In order to find a moment of shared enjoyment, they could improvise a scene when they were quite young playing with toys in the garden on a sunny day. Then they could try another improvisation when they were a bit older, say eleven or twelve, talking about clothes or boys or whatever interests girls of that age, so they could share opinions about their likes and dislikes. Another useful improvisation could be the two girls in their mid-teens having a serious discussion about their fathers. They would be at an age when they could talk to each other about their problems.

Romeo has two very close friends, Mercutio and Benvolio, but his relationship with each of these guys is quite different. Mercutio is dangerous and challenging, whereas Benvolio is rather reliable and steadfast. You can't imagine Mercutio and Benvolio getting on without Romeo being around, so what is it about Romeo that attracts both Mercutio and Benvolio? It's so easy to accept these friendships without a real understanding of their basis, but if Romeo has an improvisation with each of these two characters in turn, then the actor will find out the subtleties of difference between the two relationships. He will have to develop a part of his characterisation that appeals to Mercutio and another part that appeals to Benvolio, then he will have to unify these differences so they become part of the same person. For instance, Mercutio and Romeo could improvise a scene where they were getting drunk and having a laugh. Maybe at some sort of sporting event. And then Romeo could improvise a scene with Benvolio when they were doing some schoolwork together, or planning a trip through the countryside around Verona.

⚡ Evolving Relationships

If two or more characters have known each other for a long time then a series of improvisations can be set up to explore the ups and downs of their relationship as it has developed over the years. There will have been high times, low times, boring times and exciting times. Times full of hope and optimism and times of gloom and despair. Times of love and times of hate. These can all be explored.

If there is a married couple in a play I will usually take them through a series of improvisations. Firstly, I will ask them to improvise a date early in their relationship because that would be the time when they found each other attractive and interesting. The time when they started to fall in love. Then I often ask them to improvise the moment when they decided to get married, because that is when they elected to throw in their lot together and face the world as a partnership. If it is appropriate, I will also ask them to improvise a scene when the wife discovers she is pregnant for the first time because that is such an emotional and life-changing moment for most couples. And then I would set up another improvisation between the husband and wife when their children are toddlers, because additional members of the family can put a lot of pressure on a married couple. Depending on the plot of the play, other aspects of a couple's evolving relationship can be explored.

By the time the actors have experienced a number of these improvisations, they will have built an in-depth understanding of how their characters feel about each other.

📖 *A View from the Bridge* by Arthur Miller

In order to give a better understanding of how these relationship improvisations can be planned, I am going to go into greater detail about the ones I used rehearsing my production of *A View from the Bridge*. No two plays are alike, but if I identify the thinking behind this selection of improvisations, then it may help you to plan relationship improvisations for other plays.

Eddie and Beatrice

In order to fully understand how these two characters feel about each other I set up a series of *evolving relationship* improvisations for the actors playing this married couple.

- *Young and in love*   I asked the actors to imagine that it was a time of youthful optimism in the lives of Eddie and Beatrice when the relationship was new and romantic. I asked them to talk about their future together and to explore how it felt to be in love.

- *The new apartment*   Most of the action of the play takes place in their apartment, so I asked them to improvise the time that they first moved in together. I suggested it would be just after their wedding. A time of happiness and growing responsibility.

- *Eddie's job*   Eddie is a hard-working man, but with no real opportunity to better himself, so I asked the actors to improvise a conversation about money and work. I suggested that this might be a time when they were celebrating their second wedding anniversary so they could feel the marriage was reasonably well-established.

- *Looking after Catherine*   I asked the actors to improvise a scene where they have been married for a few years and they are discussing whether to take on the responsibility of bringing up Catherine. I asked them to think about the financial and emotional implications.

The Family

I wanted the actors playing Eddie, Beatrice and Catherine to experience various aspects of family life, so I asked them to improvise a few *family relationship* scenes together.

- *Picnic in the park* The first of these family improvisations took place when Catherine was eleven years old. I asked Eddie, Beatrice and Catherine to improvise a happy family picnic on a sunny day. No strife. No disharmony. This was to level the playing field, as it were. To give the family relationship a harmonious foundation.

- *Winter by the fire* I suggested that Catherine should now be about thirteen. A time of growing independence for a teenager. A time when children are not afraid of speaking their mind. I asked Eddie, Beatrice and Catherine to improvise an evening in winter in order to create a harsh and gloomy atmosphere. I wanted them to huddle together round the fire, but I secretly told each of them to find the other two a bit irritating so their characters could experience the feeling of claustrophobia that can sometimes happen when people get stifled in a close-knit group.

- *Sunday lunch* Eating together is often a time when members of a family talk about their life outside the family. I suggested that Catherine would now be about fifteen and her mind would be full of boys and work possibilities. I also suggested that Eddie could talk about his working life and that Beatrice should chat about her activities during the week. I wanted them to experience the fact that a family is made up of a group of individuals who all have different life experiences.

Eddie and Catherine

This relationship develops considerably during the course of the play, so I felt we needed to give it a firm foundation. A starting point. A launch pad.

- *Coney Island* I suggested that the actors improvise a scene where Eddie takes Catherine to an amusement park for her twelfth birthday. There is usually a generosity of spirit towards the person who is celebrating their birthday, so I thought that it would be a good experience for the actors since Eddie is quite tough on Catherine during the play.

- *Eddie's birthday* In order to reverse the direction of this generosity of spirit, I asked the actors to improvise a scene when Catherine is fourteen years old and greets Eddie as he gets home from work on his birthday. This echoes a scene early in the play when Catherine greets Eddie after work because she wants to tell him she's got a job and she knows he won't approve. I felt that a similar scene but without the anxiety of possible conflict would be helpful for both of the actors.

Beatrice and Catherine

This relationship is the least explored of the three during the course of the play. They have one difficult scene together where Beatrice tries to discuss the growing problem of Eddie's attraction to Catherine, but apart from that we don't know much about their relationship. I wanted to see if they could find some sort of mother/daughter bonding.

- *The prom* The school prom is an important time for American teenagers because they are celebrating a rite of passage into adulthood. They publicly shed their schooldays and become grown-ups. I asked the actors to improvise a scene where Beatrice is helping Catherine to get ready for the prom. This would remind Beatrice of her own youthful optimism and it would help her bond with Catherine. At the same time it would make Catherine feel supported and loved by Beatrice, her mother-substitute.

- *First day at college* I wanted the two actors to feel that Catherine was growing more independent, so I asked them to improvise a scene the night before Catherine starts at secretarial college. The previous improvisation was mainly about how Catherine might appeal to members of the opposite sex, so this would be more about how she might fit into the adult world of employment. Both improvisations are turning points in Catherine's life and both would be poignant self-questioning times for Beatrice as she thinks back over her own life.

Rodolpho and Marco

The other important relationship in *A View from the Bridge* is that between the two immigrants, Rodolpho and Marco. I haven't talked about them much so far, but their arrival in the apartment is the catalyst for the drama of the play because Catherine falls in love with Rodolpho.

Rodolpho is a happy-go-lucky teenage Sicilian immigrant who sees America as the golden land of opportunity, while Marco, his older married brother, has come to America in order to earn money to send back to his family. They are both wide-eyed innocents when they arrive.

In order to help the actors understand their previous lives I set up several improvisations of their lives in Sicily.

- *Marco with his family* I asked some of the actors in the company to be members of Marco's family so the actor playing Marco could improvise a scene with the family he has left behind. Marco's family is very important to him and I felt the actor needed a strong sense of who they were and what his life used to be like in Sicily.

- *Rodolpho and friends* I asked some of the other actors to become Sicilian teenage boys and girls so that the actor playing Rodolpho could improvise a scene in the village square, hanging out with his friends in the sunshine and flirting with girls.

Having given the two actors some sense of their previous life, I could now work on the relationship with one another. For this I set up a couple of improvisations:

- *Rodolpho visits Marco's family*   Using the same actors who created Marco's family, I asked them to improvise a scene where Rodolpho comes to dinner just before they both leave for America. This improvisation was to identify the difference in their hopes and expectations, but it was also useful for the actor playing Marco to discover how distracting family life can be. And, of course, it would give him a greater understanding of what he has left behind.

- *On the boat*   Finally, I asked the other actors in the company to become immigrants on the boat to America and improvise a scene in which Marco and Rodolpho could share the hopes and fears about this tremendous venture into the unknown. Although Marco and Rodolpho are very different, this improvisation helped the actors discover what their characters had in common.

Eddie and his Friends

Eddie's relationship with the outside world is another theme of the play. At the start we see him as a popular man with his workmates, and at the end of the play, his neighbours turn their back on him because he has betrayed the immigrants. Again, I wanted to build the actor's sense of his normal life so I set up the following improvisations:

- *Eddie at work*   I asked all the male actors in the group to become longshoremen with Eddie. (Some of them already had a few lines as these characters.) I then asked them to improvise a scene where they unloaded cargo from a boat. Tough work. Tough talk. Macho teasing and aggression. Sweat and swearing. Eddie's world.

- *Eddie with friends*   The final improvisation was the same group of longshoremen having a drink after work. A different atmosphere. More relaxed. Playing cards. Beer. Comrades. Friends.

Scenarios for Relationship Improvisations

When I'm devising an improvisation I don't necessarily adhere to the period setting of the production. If I think it's going to be helpful I sometimes create unashamedly anachronistic scenarios in order to allow the actors to take advantage of their own personal experience. Romeo and Mercutio on their way to a football match, for instance. Juliet and her friends getting ready to go to a disco. For me, the essence of character is not necessarily rooted in any particular era. As Shakespeare's plays reveal, many aspects of the human experience are eternal.

Although there are exceptions, asking actors to improvise their characters as children is a risky business because the whole thing can become riddled with cliché, so I wouldn't usually ask them to improvise a version of their character any younger than about eleven. That seems to me to be the age when children start to have a more adult perception of themselves and their place in the world.

I've already mentioned quite a few scenarios for these improvisations, but a checklist of suggestions may be helpful. Most of these scenarios are occasions when people are likely to be talking to each other.

- A summer picnic
- A winter's night around the fire
- With colleagues at work
- An intimate meal
- A family meal
- A birthday celebration
- A family outing
- On the beach
- Watching the sunset
- Hanging out in the street (teenage boys)
- In someone's bedroom (teenage girls)

- A walk in the park
- In the pub

Sometimes I suggest subjects for conversation, but these will be determined by the circumstances of the plot. I've already mentioned Rosalind and Celia from *As You Like It* talking about their fathers, and Juliet and her friends talking about boys. These particular topics of conversation will develop opinions, already expressed in the play, in order to give the actors a better understanding of their characters.

Finally, it's best to avoid scenarios that overwhelm the conversation, either physically – like playing tennis, chess or football – or vocally – like discussing politics, religion or the latest hit film. Unless they are directly related to the plot, these things become a distraction because they can dominate the improvisation leaving the actors no room for exploration.

It seems to me impossible to embark on a complicated play like *A View from the Bridge* without extensive exploration. The actor playing Marco could have imagined a very different version of life back in Sicily from that of the actor playing Rodolpho. In fact, they could have rehearsed the whole play with neither actor thinking much about it at all. And yet that shared experience of a previous life and a growing relationship must be at the bottom of every moment they spend together. As it must be for Eddie and Beatrice. And Eddie and Catherine. And Catherine and Beatrice. And all the characters that have known each other before the play starts.

And all the characters in all the plays that have known each other before all the plays start. Hamlet and Ophelia, Antony and Cleopatra, Hedda Gabler and Tesman, Prince Hal and Falstaff, Algernon and Ernest, Sir Toby Belch and Sir Andrew Aguecheek, Oberon and Titania. Any of them. All of them.

Let the actors create these relationships for themselves. It will give them a common vocabulary. It will make their relationships more complex and believable. It will enable them to develop a deeper shared history leading to a stronger and more captivating version of the play.

7
Centre of Attention

We all think we know who we are, but so much more is revealed when we start to talk about ourselves. I went to a Quaker meeting once because a friend of mine asked me to go. I didn't know anything about the religion, but I've always been interested in things I don't know much about. I wanted to try everything. An impossible quest, I know, but when you're young you have these ideas. The Quaker meeting was quite unlike any religious experience I had ever had before. For a start no one seemed to be in charge. We went into this smallish square room where there was a circle of chairs laid out. Other people had arrived before us and there were subliminal acknowledgements of our entrance. A nod of the head. A sideways glance. We sat down. Nothing happened. A few more people arrived. Still nothing happened. It was very quiet and peaceful, except I wasn't quite as relaxed as I might have been because I didn't know what to expect.

After we'd been sitting there for a while someone suddenly started to speak. Not actually to anyone in particular. They just spoke out loud into the room. Something about an incident that had happened to them in the street a couple of days previously. As I listened to the story I became quite involved. I was hoping to hear something about God or some sort of philosophical revelation. Or a least a punch line. A moral. Something to think about. But no. It just seemed to be about an incident on the street.

The story finished. Silence.

Then another person spoke about something else. Her kids at school or something. No morals. No message from God. No philosophy. She was just talking about herself.

Another silence.

During the session about half a dozen people talked about themselves and then it was over. My friend said that it had been a good meeting. I asked if anything else happened at other meetings. Did people testify? Did they sometimes sing hymns? No, I was told, people just talk. It helps them sort things out. It helps them understand the world. It helps

them fit in.

It's funny how just talking about ourselves can help us solve our problems. A lot of therapists and analysts just sit there and allow their clients to talk to them for fifty minutes or so. No advice is given. Sometimes there will be the odd comment to keep the ball rolling, but often the client will just talk.

And why is this?

Well, talking about yourself helps you understand who you are.

People often need to 'talk their problems through'. They will ask their friends to help them sort out their lives, but as they talk they won't let their friend get a word in edgeways. They certainly don't seem to want advice. The friend can be a great listener and sit there saying nothing for hours until finally the person with the problem says, 'Thanks for listening, it really helped' or 'Thanks for letting me talk, I feel a lot better.'

THERE'S A REHEARSAL EXERCISE CALLED 'HOT-SEATING' that is often used to explore and develop character. The actors as their characters take it in turns to be in the 'hot seat', and questions are fired at them by the other members of the cast: 'How old are you?', 'Where were you born?', etc. The actor being hot-seated has to stay in character and improvise the answers on the spot.

The point of this exercise is to force the actor to think about aspects of their character that might not have occurred to them before, and as such it can be very useful. The only trouble is that actors often get very nervous about hot-seating because they are frightened of making a mistake. In early stages of rehearsal their knowledge will obviously be quite limited and they feel as if they don't have enough information. Hopefully they will have gathered some specific facts from the script and they can use the results of their research to flesh out the background world of the play and their character's life, but they probably won't be able to remember everything, so the exercise becomes like a knowledge test. And since the rest of the cast will also have been gathering information they may be able to spot mistakes. Sometimes they will even want to correct the person being hot-seated and that just makes matters worse because the fear of getting something wrong adds to the stress.

Also, in my experience, the questions are often difficult to answer because they can be too personal. They are the sort of questions that, in real life, people wouldn't ask so bluntly. And when that happens the *actor* feels obliged to answer a question that the *character* might choose to deflect or even lie about: 'Are you cheating on your wife?' or 'Are you a homosexual?', for instance. In real life someone might not want to talk about those things, especially when they are being asked about them in front of strangers, so the whole thing starts to feel like an interrogation and the exercise becomes even more riddled with anxiety. How can anyone be creative in circumstances like that? When people are interrogated it's usually because they are suspects in a criminal investigation, so the actor being hot-seated starts to feel as if his or her character is guilty of something.

It's all rather self-defeating. Even the word 'hot-seating' sounds frightening. As if the seat is so hot it makes you want to jump up and run away. Or is it hot because the anxiety of being questioned makes you sweat with fear? Or get hot under the collar? Or be burned by the heat of an interrogation lamp? How can any of that be helpful?

No. To my mind, the best way to explore creatively is always to take away as much of the stress as possible. And the best way to do that is to make the improvisation more like real life so the actors can relax, find the truth of the situation, go with the flow, and allow things to be revealed, rather than forcing facts out under pressure.

Centre of Attention Improvisation

In what sort of real-life situation is someone asked questions about their life by several other people? Well, it can happen in a job interview, for instance. It can also happen when someone meets their boyfriend's parents for the first time. Or a person joins a tennis club and meets the other members in the bar after a game. It happens in any situation where one person becomes the centre of attention simply because the rest of the group don't know much about them.

Improvisations using this kind of scenario will help actors develop a more complex understanding of their characters without putting unnecessary pressure on them. The *character* may feel a bit stressed, but the *actor* can be relaxed. And that sets up a better environment for exploration and creativity.

Setting up a group improvisation in this way also levels the playing field and makes the process creative for everyone. The actors asking the questions will be using their acting and improvisation skills just as much as the actor who is the centre of attention. They will have to create characters, imagine a situation, develop relationships amongst themselves, and keep alert and inventive. This is much more fun, of course, but it also makes the improvisation more realistic for the actor who is being questioned.

I would suggest that a group of three or four questioners is about the right number of people to generate a variety of questions but not so many as to overwhelm the focal actor.

Choosing a Scenario

The choice of improvisation scenarios will be different for every play, and it takes quite a lot of thought to come up with suitable situations for all the different characters. Sometimes it is possible to think of an improvisation that is directly related to the play. For instance, in *Hamlet*, Laertes goes to Paris to study fencing, so it would be legitimate for him to be the centre of attention in an improvisation where he is meeting other students in a fencing academy. Maybe he's just arrived in Paris and the other students are getting to know him. They could easily want to know what it was like growing up in Denmark, or his family background, or what his life was like in Elsinore. In a modern play, an interview for an article in a magazine is often a possible scenario, especially if the character has some sort of status. In *Once in a Lifetime* by Moss Hart and George Kaufman, one of the characters becomes a successful film director, so it would be quite possible for him to be interviewed for an article in the American trade paper *Variety*.

But most of the time it is necessary to stretch the truth a little to make the improvisations fit. It can be quite fun to imagine the Ghost of Hamlet's father being interviewed by St Peter and some angels at the Pearly Gates, or Shylock being questioned about his life for an article in a Jewish newspaper. When I am working with people who are used to these techniques, I often use quite anachronistic situations. For instance, Ophelia being interviewed by *Hello!* magazine about her relationship with Prince Hamlet. Or Portia in *The Merchant of Venice* going to a dating agency to find a husband. However, once the improvisation has started, it is important that all the actors involved take it seriously, otherwise nothing is really achieved. For the people who are asking the questions, it can easily become an opportunity to create bizarre characters and have too much fun relating to each other. This makes it hard for the actor who is the centre of attention to concentrate and, as a result, he or she could start to lose focus. If this happens, I usually remind everyone that the reason they are doing these improvisations is to help each other develop their characters. They surely wouldn't want people messing around when it's their turn to be the centre of attention.

When choosing a scenario it's important not to use negative situations that can put the actor under pressure. For instance, a police interrogation would be a bad idea because the people asking the questions could get quite nasty. You should also be careful of situations where something particular has happened or is about to happen. Otherwise everyone will be distracted by specific circumstances. Being questioned by hospital staff after a car crash, for instance, would be too distracting, or an interview after a sporting event. However, an interview for a job, which in reality could be rather stressful, can be used, providing the interviewers are friendly and supportive. It's important that the improvisations are calm and relaxed.

Centre of Attention Scenarios

Some of the centre of attention scenarios that I have used in the past are where the focal character is:

- Being interviewed for an article in a newspaper or magazine (*Hello!*, *Tatler*, *The Stage*, etc.)
- Being interviewed by students from their old school who are writing an article about them in the school magazine
- Talking to total strangers (who all know each other) in an unfamiliar bar or pub
- Being interviewed to join a club (tennis, the Round Table, a men's club, the Women's Institute, etc.)
- Being questioned at a press conference
- Being interviewed on television or the radio

- At a dinner party where they don't know the other guests, but the guests all know each other
- Being interviewed for a job
- Joining a dating agency
- Answering questions from an immigration panel
- Attending a self-help group
- Meeting a girlfriend's/boyfriend's family for the first time

The Questioners

The actors asking the questions will need to give themselves characters. They can be any sort of person they like, providing it is suitable for the improvisation. They can be older, younger, intense, serious, happy-go-lucky, anything they want. These actors will be involved in a number of different centre of attention improvisations, so they can keep themselves sharp and interested by giving themselves different characters each time. The more extreme they make their characters, the more interesting it will be for the actor who is the centre of attention. Unexpected areas of knowledge will be uncovered. Although I must stress that however bizarre the questioning characters are, the actors who created them must remain faithful and true to their creations. They should never let their sense of fun overwhelm the objective of the improvisation, or distract the actor whose character is the centre of attention.

Apart from the focal character, everyone should use their own names. It's so much easier than trying to remember a whole load of made-up names. Of course, there is the danger of Leontes or Polixenes being interviewed by Jimmy, Darlene and Josh, but the positives outweigh the negatives, and when the actors take this work seriously they don't tend to be distracted by this incongruity. Perhaps it would be sensible for Jimmy and Josh to call themselves James and Joshua if they were interviewing Polixenes, but in my experience there isn't usually a problem with people using their own names.

When these improvisations are being set up it is important that each of the questioners has a specific area of interest. If it is an interview for a magazine article, for instance, then one of the interviewers could be asking about family background, another could be interested in the focal character's professional career, and a third could want to know about his or her romantic attachments. If the improvisation takes place in a bar, one questioner could want to know what the stranger (the focal character) does for a living, another could want to know about his or her leisure activities while a third could be interested in his or her childhood. Before the improvisation starts, each of the questioners should decide on their 'area of interest'.

The questioners should also all decide what the relationships are amongst themselves. Is one person the boss? Do two of the questioners hate each other? Are a couple of them married? Is one having a secret affair with one of the others? It's important that all the questioners know each other pretty well. It's equally important that none of the questioners know the focal character. If they knew them already, why would they need to ask about their lives? For instance, in the scenario when someone is meeting their girlfriend's parents for the first time, it's important that the girlfriend isn't one of the questioners. She could be late home from work or something, so the focal character is meeting all the questioners (her family) for the first time.

The improvisation should never feel like hot-seating. Obviously, in an interview, the interview panel will be asking direct questions, but they can also talk amongst themselves. In fact, they *should* talk amongst themselves. One person may be the centre of attention, but that doesn't mean that other people in the improvisation can't have discussions or even separate conversations.

Depending on the characters they have chosen, the questioners can be helpful, friendly or even flirty, but above all they should find a reason for wanting to know about the focal character without it becoming an interrogation.

It's best to arrange any seating in an informal manner so that the focal character becomes part of the group. Sitting in a circle or sitting around a table is far less intimidating than being faced by a row of questioners.

Being the Centre of Attention

The actor who is exploring their character by being the centre of attention in these improvisations should take a few moments to 'become' their character using the techniques discussed in previous chapters. I usually send them out of the room for a few minutes before the improvisation starts so they can get focused and prepared.

Once the improvisation starts, the actor at the centre of attention should behave exactly as they think their character would behave. They don't have to answer difficult questions if they don't want to, but if they refuse, they should decline to answer in a manner that is suitable for their character. The purpose of these improvisations is to get the actors to think about things they haven't previously considered. The character may decline to answer the question, or they might answer the question with a lie, but the actor playing the part will consider the question and secretly know the answer.

Also, it doesn't matter if the actor playing the focal character gets something wrong. As I said, at this stage in rehearsals they won't be able to remember everything, and one or two mistakes are perfectly all right and they should be ignored. Nothing will be gained by stopping and correcting things; all that will happen is that the actor will feel stupid and distracted, and that could make them inhibited. Similarly, if the questioners get something wrong that too should be ignored. Mistakes can be identified after the improvisation has finished.

These improvisations work on two levels. Not only do they force the actors to think about their characters and flesh them out, they also give the actors a chance just to be their characters for an extended period of time in situations that are only loosely connected to the play. After the improvisation has been going on for a while, the actors will start to relax. They should take a leaf out of John Wayne's acting method. He said, 'I don't act… I react', and that's what the centre of attention improvisation is all about.

I have found that these improvisations work best if they are about fifteen to twenty minutes long. This will give everyone a chance to settle down and become familiar with the improvisation and still leave plenty of time for unexpected detours.

Post-improvisation Discussion

It's important to discuss the improvisation afterwards, so everyone can identify both the productive discoveries and the unhelpful mistakes. The actor who was the centre of attention can talk about aspects of the improvisation which were revealing and helpful, while the questioners can feed back interesting things about the focal character that they observed during the improvisation.

After these intensive explorations, everyone should have a strong sense of who their characters are and how they feel about other people. They will have learned how to 'think' like their characters and they will have discovered how their characters behave when dealing with a variety of different people. This will give the actors a solid foundation to work from as they start to use the text of the play and rehearse the scenes.

8

Sense Memory

I can't stand it when a complete maniac in a drugged-up state points a gun at the hero, and the hero makes some sort of wise-crack. I'm talking about movies here. I mean, I've only had a gun pointed in my direction once and that was an air gun from fifty yards away outside my office window. A middle-class West London teenager had gone out on his parent's balcony to see if he could pot a pigeon or break a neighbour's window and he noticed I was looking at him. As he turned and pointed the gun at me I ducked. Pretty fast. Actually, I was furious that he had threatened me, although I knew he was just messing about. My skin had contracted with fear and the hairs stood up on the back of my neck.

I called the police.

They arrived in about two seconds flat.

Complete with bullet-proof vests and crackling radios.

They took the whole thing very seriously, crawling on their hands and knees towards the window and peering over the sill with just their eyes. They knew what guns can do. I didn't and I was scared. They did and they certainly weren't making wise-cracks.

Of course, it turned out to be nothing, but the thing that strikes me is that it takes so little effort to pull the trigger. When a totally out-of-control pathological nutcase is pointing a gun at you, he hardly has to do anything to send you spinning into eternity. Even if he didn't mean to do it.

Someone drew a knife on me for real once and I was absolutely terrified. Dry mouth. Clenched stomach. Weak knees. The lot. I had no idea what to say, let alone make a joke or even try to reason with him. My mind went completely blank. All I wanted to do was run away.

Heroes are different. They're used to danger. But surely they are scared of dying just like the rest of us. Surely the adrenalin surges into their muscles the same way it does for us ordinary people.

Stop all this wise-cracking, say I. Find the truth of the situation – it'll be so much more effective.

There were a couple of young special agents on TV in the seventies called Bodie and Doyle. Anyone remember? *The Professionals.* They drove around in Ford Escorts and fired guns at criminals. Bodie was your archetypal brave hero who looked tough,

clenched his jaw and was positively fearless as he went on dangerous missions. Doyle was different. He always looked a little terrified and slightly confused. When he stepped out from behind a protective rubbish skip to take a shot at the baddy, you could see it in his eyes. He was scared stiff. He was brave but he knew that the consequences could be disastrous. The funny thing was, being aware of the dangers and yet still facing psychopaths with weapons made Doyle seem even more heroic than Bodie.

Interestingly, Martin Shaw, the actor who played Doyle, had been viciously attacked by muggers when he was younger and they'd broken his cheekbone so badly that it had to be replaced by a plastic plate.

Maybe it was the memory of that experience that brought a sense of reality to his dealings with violence in *The Professionals.* He remembered feeling weak at the knees. He remembered how his heart pounded. He remembered the shortness of breath and the clenched stomach. He remembered the fear of danger and he was able to use that sense memory when he acted.

A LOT OF THE TIME ACTORS HAVE TO DO THINGS ON STAGE and screen that they have never actually done in their own lives. How does it feel the moment before you take a sleeping potion that will make everyone think you're dead? Well, Juliet has to do it but I doubt that any actress who has played Juliet has ever had the experience herself. So what does an actress do in a situation like that? She uses her imagination. She imagines what it might be like and goes from there.

The only trouble is that the imagination isn't that reliable. Reality is often a bit different. Have you ever arrived at a holiday destination to discover that your hotel room is nothing like you had imagined it? Ever seen a fantastic chocolate cream cake and imagined how it would taste, only to be totally disappointed when you bit into it? See what I mean? Totally unreliable. So, in order to get a more accurate version of your expectations, the imagination needs a bit of help from real experience.

When Stanislavsky was trying to analyse and identify what goes on in the creative minds of actors, he realised that one of the hardest things they have to do is find the truth in the emotional reaction to an incident that they have never actually experienced themselves. However, he felt that the problem could be solved if actors were to recall their emotional reaction to comparable incidents from their own lives. The exercises that Stanislavsky created to address this problem have been variously translated as Emotional Memory, Affective Memory or Sense Memory. There is a minefield of conflicting theories about all this, but as I understand it, the actor has to recollect an incident from their own lives and relive the ensuing emotion as they play a scene. If a character has to experience the death of a friend, but the actor has never experienced that in his or her life, then perhaps the memory of a pet that died when the actor was a child may be used to recreate the sensation of that emotional experience.

It seems like a good idea. If an actor is playing a love scene and has to look into the eyes of a stage lover, then remembering a *real* experience of love with a *real* lover makes it easier for them to recreate the right emotions.

When actors are acting, they can often start to feel as if the situation they are going through is actually happening. The mind is a funny thing. Perhaps that's why film stars are always falling in love with each other and cheating on their husbands and wives. Two actors will play a love scene so truthfully that they start to believe it's real. They think that they are falling in love because they seem to be sharing the experience of falling in love. They then throw caution to the wind and start to date off-screen. And before they know it, they are in the middle of an affair. (Six months after the filming has finished, the affair is over too. Such is the life of a film star.)

So if the experience of 'acting' love can have such a powerful impact on the emotion of an actor, why not use improvisation to create *imaginary* emotional memories? The actor doesn't have to remember a time when his cat died in order to find the right emotion for the death of his character's best friend. He can improvise a scene where the friend dies in his arms and if both actors are emotionally involved in the improvisation, the actor can use the memory of that improvisation to recreate the right emotional state for his character.

Something like this happened when I was working on *Someone Who'll Watch Over Me* (see Chapter 4: Preparing a Character). You will remember that during a series of improvisations about the hostage-takers I told the guards, without any warning, that they were to take out one of the hostages from each cell to be shot. At the time, the actors playing the guards were genuinely shocked by the experience. Later in rehearsals they were able to use the memory of that improvisation when they played a similar scene. No one is actually taken out to be shot in *Someone Who'll Watch Over Me*, but there is a scene where two of the hostages are left alone in the cell after the third hostage has been executed.

⚡ Sharing a Sense Memory

In Tennessee Williams's play *Period of Adjustment*, two of the male characters had been young soldiers during the Korean War. The action of the play takes place several years after the war, during which time the two characters haven't seen each other. However, the shared experience of being in battle had been tremendously bonding for them. When I was rehearsing this play I decided that it would be a good idea to try to recreate a battle experience, so I set up an improvisation where the two characters were supposed to be in a muddy foxhole together, talking about their lives, girls, what they felt about war, etc. We decided that they should imagine they had a rifle each, some food and a machine gun set up at the edge of the foxhole.

When they were ready, they started the improvisation.

I let it progress for a while, but I could tell it wasn't working properly. It just seemed to be two guys talking about their lives. The conversation could have happened anywhere. At university. In a bar. Walking down the street. There was nothing happening to make the experience particularly bonding, because there was no sense of shared danger. Their lives weren't on the line.

So, as I let them carry on with the improvisation, I secretly instructed the other actors in the room to get ready to make the sound of a battle. A couple of them found some pieces of wood that they would be able to rattle along the old cast-iron radiators to make the sound of machine guns. Some of the others got chairs they could bang on the top of wooden rostra to give the effect of big explosions. Other people found other bits of wood that they could snap against the floor to sound like rifle shots. They didn't try any of these out, of course, because we wanted to surprise the improvisers.

I often have several things happening in a rehearsal room at the same time, so the two improvisers didn't notice any of this silent preparation. They just carried on improvising their scene.

When the rest of the actors were ready, I gave the signal for them to start making the noise of an attack. It was brilliant. We had no idea how it would turn out – but it worked. It sounded terrifying. It was very loud and violent. Much better than I could have hoped.

The two actors were extremely shocked. They went into a blind panic as they tried to pick up their imaginary rifles. They struggled with the imaginary machine gun and started trying to fire back. It was so loud they had to shout at each other to be heard, and they were totally confused because they hadn't anticipated the attack and didn't know where it was coming from. They could only hear the noise. You could see that the adrenalin was pumping for real.

After a few minutes I gave the signal to stop the attack and the noise died down. Luckily, the actors that I work with know that they should never stop an improvisation until I tell them to, so after the attack, the two guys carried on improvising.

This time there was an edge. Part of their attention was outside the foxhole as they talked. I kept the other actors on standby with their pieces of wood and rostra and chairs, so the two improvisers couldn't tell if there was going to be another attack or not. There wasn't, but I let the improvisation continue for a while with the tension and fear of death hanging over them as they spoke.

After it was over, the two actors said that the attack had been terrifying and they really began to feel what it might have been like on a genuine battlefield. Neither I nor any of the actors had experienced war, but we began to get some sort of sense of how it might feel in such a life-threatening situation.

When the two actors eventually rehearsed the scene where they meet up for the first time as civilians, they were able to use the memory of that shared experience and it helped them create the truth behind the wild excitement and mutual understanding that old war-buddies seem to have for each other.

Physical Sense Memory

When I was an actor I was in a stage adaptation of a short story by Nathanael West called *Miss Lonelyhearts*. I had to play a character called Peter Doyle who is severely handicapped. In the script he is described as a cripple. Actually, he is also described as being inarticulate because he has difficulty speaking so I didn't have many lines to learn. However, Peter Doyle is a tremendously important character in the play and I had lots of time in rehearsals to think about how I was going to become a convincing inarticulate cripple.

I don't know why, but children often like to pretend they've got a limp, so I started messing around with versions of the limps I had tried out as a boy. None of them seemed to work. My Douglas Bader walk seemed phoney. (Douglas Bader was the Second World War flying ace who lost both his legs in an air crash — brilliantly played by Kenneth Moore in the film *Reach for the Sky*.) Then I realised that people who have a physical disability don't try to walk with a limp. They try to walk straight. It is the disability that causes them to walk the way they do. Or the pain. Not a desire to limp. So I thought that I would use that idea as a starting point and create a disability for myself.

First of all, I put some pebbles in one of my shoes and tried walking around like that. It hurt, but I tried not to let it affect the way I moved. I got pretty good at covering up the pain and began to realise that that is what disabled people sometimes do. They try to disguise the pain they are experiencing.

The next thing I decided was that I wanted to have a knee that didn't bend, so I tied a piece of wood to my leg from ankle to thigh, like a sort of splint, and then tried walking with that. It was very difficult to disguise the limp this time, because I had to swing my leg out sideways as I walked to stop it jamming into the ground. As I practised, I discovered that I didn't have to swing the leg out sideways so much if I lifted up my hip as I brought the leg forward. If I did that then my 'disability' was hardly noticeable.

Finally I decided to try taping up my other knee with duct tape so it would always be slightly bent.

The pebbles, the splint and the taped-up knee. It sounds a lot, but the point was that I was trying to walk normally with all these restrictions, not trying to walk with a limp.

By the time the play went into performance I didn't have to use any of the strapping-up devices to create the effect of a disability, I could use the sense memory of the work I had done with various restrictions, and remember how it affected the way I felt and consequently the way I walked.

People told me that I was totally convincing in the part. Thank goodness for that. But by the time we were performing the play, the physicality of the character had become second nature, so I didn't have to think about it. At all. I just played the scenes concentrating on my objectives, emotions and stuff like that without even thinking about the limp. I'm convinced that this is how people with disabilities lead their lives.

Emotional Memory

The characters in *Someone Who'll Watch Over Me* go through an experience that is totally alien to the life experiences of the actors playing them, so when we were rehearsing the play I felt it was necessary to explore some of the events through improvisation. What was it like to be kidnapped? What was it like to be bundled into the boot of a car and prodded with a rifle? What was it like to wear a blindfold for weeks on end? What was it like to be in a cell that was so small you could touch both the side walls at the same time if you stretched out your arms? What was it like to be totally under the control of people with guns who didn't care whether you lived or died?

Before rehearsing the play we had all read Brian Keenan's book about the hostage crisis (*An Evil Cradling*) and John McCarthy's book about the same thing, which he wrote with Jill Morrell (*Some Other Rainbow*). Both books describe their emotional journeys in great detail, so we had some idea of what they had undergone. I thought that it was important for the actors to experience some of these hardships and fears for themselves. As I mentioned earlier, although *Someone Who'll Watch Over Me* only has three characters, I worked on it with about eighteen students all acting in different scenes, so I was able to devise group improvisations which proved to be useful for all involved. Also, I didn't want the actors to be the characters in the play for these exercises and improvisations; I wanted them to try to have the experience *as themselves*, so they could discover truthful reactions.

A Game of Oppression

First of all, we played a game which is an adaptation of an Augusto Boal exercise. Everyone stood in a circle, shoulder to shoulder with their eyes shut, except for one person who walked around the outside of the circle banging a rolled-up newspaper into the palm of their hand to make an aggressive noise. At any time the person with the rolled-up newspaper could hit a victim across the shoulders. When this happened, the victim had to open their eyes and run clockwise round the outside of the circle while the person with the newspaper chased them, trying to hit them with it again and again. Everyone else had to keep their eyes shut the whole time. After one circuit, the hitter handed the rolled-up newspaper to the victim, joined the circle and shut their eyes. The person who now held the newspaper became the next hitter and the whole thing started again.

After a few circuits I secretly stopped the current hitter and victim, took them to one side and told them both to become hitters. I gave them each a rolled-up newspaper and they went back to the circle. The people with their eyes shut were confused because they didn't know there were two hitters now, and to start with they found it hard to work out what was happening.

After a couple more circuits I secretly whispered to the next pair of hitters that they should talk to each other in gobbledegook (nonsense language) as they walked around the circle hitting the newspaper in the palm of their hands.

When doing this exercise it was important that everyone in the circle kept their eyes shut the whole time when they were not involved in either hitting or running, because that built up a feeling of uncertainty and powerlessness.

When we sat down to discuss this exercise, people said that the longer it went on, the more unnerving it was. They also said, surprisingly, that they felt pleased when they heard someone else being chased because they were glad it wasn't them. The most frightening time was when the person next to you was suddenly hit and chased because the danger was too close for comfort. The general feeling was that it was much better to be a hitter than a victim.

Blindfolds

Before I started this series of improvisations, I warned all the actors that they should be very careful not to let anyone get hurt, because it involved a certain amount of manhandling.

Firstly, we blindfolded half the actors, moved them around the room to disorientate them and then made them sit on the floor. Then I silently indicated to the other actors that they should follow me out of the room. Once we were in the corridor I explained that I wanted people to work in pairs, moving the blindfolded actors around the room. I showed them a way to hold someone that would be firm and safe, by taking hold of an upper arm and an elbow each. I explained that they should go back in the room and start moving the blindfolded actors around. They should pick one of them up, run them swiftly to another part of the room and sit them down without saying anything. Having moved one person they could pick out another one and do the same.

Once it started there was immediately a sense of fear in the room. Some of the blindfolded actors hated being made to run across the room. They were terrified that they would run into something, so there was a great deal of anxiety. Of course, they were perfectly safe, but they didn't feel as if they were. I then silently indicated that we should leave the room so the blindfolded actors were left alone again.

Once in the corridor I told them that they should move people around in the same way, but this time they should burst angrily into the room shouting gobbledegook to each other as if they were speaking a foreign language.

This was even more effective because the noise and sense of anger escalated the fear and confusion of the blindfolded actors.

We did the same exercise a third time, but when we were in the corridor, I asked the actors to stroll into the room laughing and having casual gobbledegook conversations. When they moved the blindfolded people around they had to whisper comforting gobbledegook in their ears.

It was unnerving for the actors who were blindfolded.

Finally, I told the actors in the corridor that they could choose any of the versions we had practised. Silence. Shouting angrily. Laughing. Or with comforting whispers. And they should mix it all up a bit as they held the blindfolded actors firmly by the arms and either made them run or walk around the room. I also said they could make unexpected noises by banging chairs on the floor, or hitting their palms with rolled-up newspapers to make the blindfolded actors jump. It so happened that we were rehearsing in a room on the ground floor so we were able to march some of them outside into a back alley of the building and just leave them there for a while. During these improvisations, the blindfolded actors often just sat still, hoping that no one would pick on them as they listened to the others being bullied and rushed about.

After a while I silently indicated that the blindfolded actors should be left sitting in pairs near each other and then we all pretended to leave the room. We huddled by the door and watched for a long time. The blindfolded actors didn't know we were still there and they were waiting for us to burst back in again and do something horrible. One by one they realised that another person was sitting near them. Some of them reached out to touch the other person. There was some tentative whispering. A couple huddled together.

After a while I stopped the improvisation and we had a long discussion.

Most of the blindfolded actors felt that it was a horrible experience, despite the fact that they knew it was their friends who were moving them about. They pointed out that it would have been much worse if they had been at the mercy of aggressive strangers holding Kalashnikovs and shouting at them in a foreign language.

The discussion went on for a long time and there were some interesting discoveries. They said that after a while they became immune to what was going on. They felt so helpless, so lacking in control that they stopped reacting to the dangers. They just let themselves be manhandled as they retreated into their own minds and thoughts.

They also said that they were often completely disorientated. Especially when they were taken into the back alley and left there. They knew they were outside but they had no idea where they were.

During the last section, when they were left on their own for a long time while we watched, they kept thinking that another assault was about to happen. The actors at the far end of the room thought we really had left the room, although some of the actors near the door suspected we were still there. The anxiety and uncertainty had stopped them wanting to communicate with each other.

It was very revealing. The blindfolded actors realised that the thought of an imminent assault would be in the back of the hostages' minds all the time they were in the cells, and that would affect the way they behaved, whatever else they may be doing.

They finally said that before the improvisations they had had no idea how frightening the experience of being a hostage would have been.

In order for the other half of the group to have a similar experience, I repeated the improvisation. However, I had to make some unexpected alterations in order to give them the same sense of uncertainty and anxiety.

Talking in Their Cells

I spent one whole morning with groups just 'being in their cells', so they would at least get some idea of the boredom that the hostages also felt. First of all, I asked them to set up chairs to create the space of a cell. Through our research we had some idea of the size of these cells. In fact, they were very small.

When they had created their cells, I asked them to imagine that they themselves had been locked up in them and that they had been there for three months. I told them that I would be suggesting various things to them but that they should try to keep their minds focused on 'being in the cell' while I talked. To start with, I left them for a while so they could get in the mood.

Once that seemed to be established I asked them to start having a conversation about food. They could describe meals. They could tell the others about their favourite food. They could imagine the taste and texture of particular things they liked and try to describe them to the others. They just had to talk about food.

I let that carry on for about fifteen minutes and then I asked them to tell each other about the place where they grew up. What their town was like. Their school. The house they lived in. I asked them to be as descriptive and detailed as possible.

I reminded them that they should stay in the improvisation all the time, even when I gave them instructions, so they could keep their imaginations rolling.

Next, I asked them to talk about the people they themselves loved. Then I asked them to entertain each other with stories from their own lives. I got them to tell each other jokes, to find each other irritating, to think of something physical that they could do together, and to tell each other something they had never told anyone else.

Each of these topics lasted about fifteen minutes, so they were in the cells without a break for several hours. During that time the atmosphere in the room kept changing. Sometimes it was quite jolly. At other times it was serious and emotional.

The point of these improvisations is to give the actors different physical and emotional experiences that are related to the action of the play. They will then be able to use the memory of their own emotional reactions in order to fully understand the feelings of the characters they are playing. By using their imagination and their commitment to truth, they will give themselves emotional reference points that can be used later on in the rehearsal process. There are no hard and fast rules on how to do this, but I would suggest that the improvisations should be based around the emotional and/or physical life-experience that would have affected and formed the personality and temperament of the characters.

The Glass Menagerie by Tennessee Williams

Laura has a clubbed foot, is very shy and she is convinced she is unattractive to men. This could be for a number of reasons, but it seems likely that her mother has been overbearing as Laura was growing up, and Laura has been unable to live up to her mother's expectations. Also, the other children at Laura's school probably bullied her because of her disability. We can't be sure, but we do know that one of the other pupils – Jim O'Connor – was nice to her one time in class and she remembers the occasion and has been in love with him ever since. This would indicate that the other pupils didn't treat her very well.

In order to give the actress a sense memory of a disastrous childhood, an exercise could be set up where the other actors – particularly the actress playing Laura's mother – could ask the actress playing Laura to attempt impossible tasks. For instance, she could be asked to do fifty press-ups, or balance a broomstick on one hand while bouncing a ball with the other. She could be asked to write a sonnet on a subject she doesn't know much about or complete a difficult Sudoku in a short space of time. When she fails at these tasks, the other actors could undermine her attempts and tell her how useless she is, and how much better other people are at doing things.

There could also be an extended improvisation where everyone is at school and all the other pupils bully the actress playing Laura and laugh at her, particularly drawing attention to her disability.

It is important to establish a safe and supportive environment in the rehearsal room before embarking on an improvisation like this because the actress playing Laura has to experience this as herself, not as her character in the play. She needs to

---

experience the humiliation that Laura has endured so she can fully understand the emotional inner life of her character, but ultimately the actress herself must feel secure and amongst friends. As I have said before, actors have the ability to immerse themselves in imaginative situations, but they also need to be given the opportunity to separate these from reality. After having experienced the humiliation of her character, the actress needs to understand that she herself is supported and liked by the rest of the cast.

9

Creating a History

When I was about ten or eleven I started to learn French. Our French teacher was called Mr Parry – think about it: 'Paree'… Paris. Isn't it funny how people's names sometimes suit their jobs? Is that because kids tease each other when they are very young and the connection is made? 'Harry Lamb, you should be a butcher when you grow up! Tee hee hee!' 'Lamb, lamb, butcher man!' Mr Parry looked like Dracula. He swept his black hair back from his forehead and strode down the corridor with his gown billowing out like bat wings. (Teachers wore gowns in those days. Well, they did at my school.)

During one of my early French lessons I had to stand up in class and say a sentence I had constructed in French. 'No, no,' said Mr Parry. 'That's all wrong.' I was disappointed, but through my disappointment a thought occurred to me. 'But, Mr Parry,' I plucked up the courage. 'If I said it like that to a Frenchman, would he understand me?' Dracula's little red eyes narrowed and he fixed me with his stare. 'That's not the point,' he snarled. At that moment the classroom door opened and a stranger in a suit came into the room. He was a school inspector. Mr Parry pointed at me as I stood at my desk and said to the inspector: '*Un garçon stupide.*' I understood that all right. I wanted to sink through the floor.

A couple of years earlier my mum took me to Warner's Holiday Camp on the Isle of Wight. Uncle Dave looked after all the little kids during the week while the grown-ups lay round the pool, had tennis tournaments or stayed indoors playing cards because of the rain.

Each week Uncle Dave got all the kids to put on a show. We rehearsed sketches, songs and dances and performed them on the Friday evening. He taught us a song called 'If I Were Not Upon the Stage', and we each had a verse to sing with a different occupation. I was to be a barrow boy. My verse went like this:

If I were not upon the stage,
Someone else I'd like to be.
If I were not upon the stage,
A barrow boy I'd be.
You'd hear me all day long,
Singing out this song,
'Ripe bananas, ripe bananas,
Only a penny a pound.

Ripe bananas, ripe bananas,
Only a penny a pound.'

When it came to the performance, I shouted out my last four lines like a real market trader, being particularly proud of my cockney accent on the word 'pound'. It brought the house down. Everyone loved my barrow boy. They laughed and they cheered and they clapped me more than anyone else. I loved it.

These two incidents had a strong effect on my life. Despite being a pretty good student in all other subjects, I was hopeless at French. Never could master it. I was terrified to get it wrong. But being on the stage! What joy! I didn't know it at the time, but the reason the grown-ups at Warner's Holiday Camp cheered and shouted was because I sang my verse hopelessly out of tune. But who cares! They loved me! Far better to be loved by a crowd of grown-ups than to be an isolated, confused *garçon stupide* in front of a school inspector in a suit.

I went on the stage.

PAST EXPERIENCES, LARGE OR SMALL, CAN AFFECT US FOR the rest of our lives. They make us who we are, and as a result we are all fascinated by our own personal history. Psychoanalysts and therapists often ask us to remember our childhood and search for moments that may have caused joy or trauma. Who are we? Where do we come from? Eternal questions. We all want to know the answers. Even recent experiences can have a long-lasting effect on us for the rest of our lives.

I sometimes find that a series of improvisations around particular events in a character's past can be helpful when an actor is trying to understand the emotions and actions of that character as they are revealed during the action of the play.

These improvisations are similar to relationship improvisations in that they often involve other characters in the play, but the difference is that they highlight specific events that may have caused emotional or even traumatic reactions in the characters. When the actors improvise these events they will discover how their characters dealt with them, and how they may have been affected by them for the rest of their lives. These can be occasions that are referred to during the action of the play, either directly or obliquely. But they don't have to be. The director can make them up.

These improvisations won't be useful for all plays, and I don't always use them, but it's worth explaining how they work to see if they would add anything to the play you are working on.

Creating a History

Sometimes the action of a scene is the result of several events that may have happened over a number of weeks or even years. These events are not part of the action of the play, but through improvisation, the actors can experience them for themselves to develop a deeper understanding of their recent history. This is particularly useful if the characters have known each other for a long time.

Period of Adjustment by Tennessee Williams

The action of the play takes place over a few hours, during which time we learn a lot about what has happened to all the characters in the past. Ralph is married to his boss's daughter, Dorothea, and his father-in-law now hates him. But it hasn't always been this way. The relationship has developed and changed considerably over the years. When the couple first met, Ralph had just returned from fighting in the Korean War and was considered to be a war hero. We learn from the dialogue that Dorothea's father, Mr McGill, must have been quite impressed when Ralph started to work for him. He even promoted him after a couple of years and suggested that one day he would run the business. In fact, it gradually transpires that Dorothea's father even suggested to Ralph that he should marry his daughter. But Ralph hated working for Mr McGill and felt he was trapped in his marriage to Dorothea. He started drinking and eventually quit his job. Just before the play starts, Dorothea has left Ralph and gone back to live with her parents. Her father is furious with Ralph, but Ralph doesn't care. Towards the end of the play, Dorothea's father confronts Ralph. It's the only scene they have together in the play, but, this being a Tennessee Williams play, the scene is complex and dynamic.

When I directed the play I felt that the actors really needed to have an understanding of the way the relationship between Ralph and Dorothea's father, Mr McGill, had developed, so I set up a sequence of improvisations, using as much information from the script as I could.

- *The returning war hero* – still wearing his uniform (imagined in the improvisation), Ralph has an interview with Mr McGill for a job. Setting – McGill's office.

- *Promotion* – after Ralph has become a good employee, Mr McGill promotes him. Setting – McGill's office.

- *A future son-in-law* – Mr McGill suggests that Dorothea would make a good wife for Ralph. Setting – a bar in McGill's exclusive golf club.

- *False expectations* – Mr McGill's speech at the wedding. Ralph is uncomfortable. Setting – the wedding reception.

- *The unhappy husband* – Ralph and Dorothea visit her parents with their new baby. Ralph is drinking too much and Dorothea isn't happy. Setting – the McGills' house.

- *Breaking the bonds* – Ralph tells Mr McGill that he is quitting his job. Setting – McGill's office.

- *Dorothea leaves* – Ralph and Dorothea have a fight and she leaves him. Setting – Ralph and Dorothea's house.

- *Running back to Daddy* – Dorothea tells her parents that she has left Ralph and why. Setting – the McGills' house.

This set of improvisations for *Period of Adjustment* explored the developing relationship between Ralph and Mr McGill, but the actors had also worked on some relationship improvisations between Dorothea and her father, between Mr and Mrs McGill, and between Dorothea and Ralph, so by the time they came to rehearse the final confrontation scene, everyone knew exactly who their characters were and what they felt about each other. They had experienced the build-up and subsequent decay of the evolving relationships, so they were able to tap into a network of changing moods and emotions. When McGill calls Ralph a 'war hero' during the confrontation scene, the phrase is weighed down with irony and sarcasm. But both the actors had experienced, through improvisation, a time when the phrase had been used to flatter and praise, and the memory of that improvisation added an edge to both the actor playing McGill, who spat the phrase out, and the actor playing Ralph, who couldn't help but be aware of the changing emphasis.

I always plan a series of improvisations like this in advance of rehearsals, but it would be equally valuable to create them through discussion with the actors by asking them what they think they need. Sometimes an improvisation can throw up unexpected bits of information that need to be examined in more detail. An actor could discover that their character responds to an incident in an improvisation rather violently, and they may want to explore the source of that repressed anger in another improvisation. Maybe two characters find they have more in common than they thought, and the actors may want to take that discovery further.

The Norman Conquests by Alan Ayckbourn

This trilogy of plays takes place at Annie's house when her brother and sister, Reg and Ruth, come to stay for the weekend with their respective partners, Sarah and Norman. Annie's friend Tom is there too, although he isn't, strictly speaking, Annie's partner. He has been in love with Annie for a long time but he's hopelessly unable to do anything about it. These six people have spent time together on a regular basis over the preceding years, so a series of improvisations to explore their developing relationships would be extremely valuable. How did the siblings behave with each other when they were teenagers? Who was the first to introduce their new partner to the others? How do each of the siblings react to these new additions to the family? How did the partners react to each other in the past?

The following improvisations would help the actors explore and establish the complexities of the character's relationships:

- The siblings, Reg, Ruth and Annie, as teenagers.
- The first time one of the siblings introduces their new partner (probably Reg introducing Sarah).
- Several years ago. Reg and Sarah visit Annie for the weekend and Tom (Annie's hopeless admirer) drops by for a meal.
- Ruth introducing her new boyfriend Norman to her brother and sister for the first time.
- All six at Christmas, five years ago.
- All six at Easter, two years ago.

Of course, a series of improvisations like this would be a major piece of work in their own right, but the relationships between the six people in *The Norman Conquests* are the crux of the whole play, so it is worth spending quite a lot of time exploring them in detail. After completing these improvisations, the actors would have developed a good understanding of the complexity and subtlety of feeling that the characters have for each other. They will know the ups and downs of the relationships because they will have actually experienced some of them.

Improvisations like these can be useful, but with a limited rehearsal period it is important to make sure that the work is beneficial to the action of the play. Sometimes actors can get carried away and want to improvise all sorts of things that may be interesting but have no relevance to the events that they have to portray onstage in front of an audience. I would advise any director using these methods to make sure that all the improvisations are closely connected to the plot. Having said that, with enough rehearsal time there are plenty of useful and informative improvisations that support and illuminate the text of any play. These will help the actors to develop a greater insight into the way their characters think and behave, and as a result they will reveal a true understanding of the complexity and unpredictability of human behaviour. And that is drama.

10

Preparing to Rehearse

In the early eighties I was lucky enough to get a job filming a commercial on the streets of New York. I was there for ten days, stayed in the Grand Hyatt Hotel, earned loads of money and saw a different show every night. Broadway musicals. Classic revivals and Off-Broadway hits. It was great. One show that I went to see was *Balm in Gilead* by Lanford Wilson at the Circle Repertory Theatre. It was presented by the Steppenwolf Theatre Ensemble, directed by John Malkovich and starred Gary Sinise. You can see why it attracted my attention.

The play was set in and around an all-night café in New York and was peopled with a variety of heroin addicts, prostitutes and thieves. There was a lot of overlapping dialogue and simultaneous scenes. The action swirled, simmered and exploded with a cast of about thirty actors rushing in and out, laughing and fighting, or just hanging around. Amazingly enough, it was quite possible to keep focus and concentrate on the relevant action despite the continual background activity. That was until halfway through the second act when a fight broke out. Someone got punched and everyone on stage started shouting and running back and forth and grabbing people. They were improvising dialogue and making up their moves on the spot as the action built to its frenzied climax. Suddenly the blade of a knife flashed and a body dropped to the ground. Dead. Blackout. Silence.

A few seconds later when the lights came up, the whole cast was running around and shouting again, but the audience soon realised that the action had gone back in time about one minute. The fight was breaking out all over again. People were shouting and grabbing each other exactly as they had before. The improvised dialogue and activity were precisely as they had been the first time. It hadn't been improvised at all. The second version was a perfect repeat of the first. The blade flashed, the body

dropped to the ground. Blackout. Silence.

The lights came up a third time. The whole fight in all its detail was repeated yet again right up to the point of death and then the scene continued. It was a fabulous moment of theatre.

But what made it so interesting was the fact that you could piece together the progression of the fight more clearly with each repeat. You could examine the details of the action right up until the moment of death and that gave a clearer understanding of why and how it had happened. It was a bit like watching a slow-motion repeat of a moment of sports action. You couldn't change the outcome, but you could gain a greater insight into the circumstances leading up to it.

ALL THE IMPROVISATIONS SO FAR HAVE BEEN ABOUT character and relationships, and although the play itself has been the inspiration behind the work, I haven't really talked about how to rehearse the actual scenes.

Learning the Lines

When I am directing a play, I spend the first few days examining the text with the whole cast as described in Chapters 1 to 3, and then for the next week or so I set up improvisations to develop character and explore their relationships, as described in Chapters 4 to 7. During this time I will also have asked the actors to learn their lines. I never ask the actors to start rehearsing a scene with their scripts in their hands. I always think that's just reading standing up. To me, an important aspect of acting is communication, and I don't think actors can communicate with each other if they are holding a couple of scripts between them. The scripts become a barrier to communication. I believe it's far better for actors to look each other in the eye as they talk, even if they are still struggling to remember the words.

There are several dangers to working this way. For a start, some older actors will say, 'I can't learn my lines until I know my moves.' But I don't see why not. And anyway, the moves should come from the desires and objectives that a character feels during a scene and those can't properly be understood until the actors are actually acting the scene. I know this could be construed as a chicken and egg situation, but isn't all of the rehearsal process like that? At any point you are only able to rehearse with the things you have learned so far. You've got to start somewhere. So for those actors who say they can't learn their lines until they know their moves, I say: please try it; it could change your way of working. Yes, it's tough, but it's tremendously liberating. The sooner actors can start 'playing' a scene, the more time they will have for creative experimentation.

There is another danger that occurs when actors learn their lines in isolation: they learn them with particular inflections which have nothing to do with the way someone else in the scene may be saying their lines. That's a difficult problem to overcome. But look at it this way: in the traditional method of working, actors are often perfectly satisfied if they don't get all their lines right until the dress rehearsal, or even the first night! A lot of the rehearsal period is taken up with actors trying to remember half-learned scripts and what a waste of creative time that is. All the director can do is sit and watch the struggle. In fact, I tell the actors I work with that I won't rehearse a scene if they haven't learned their lines properly. I don't get cross with them, I just rehearse another scene. If that goes on for a couple of days, the actors learn their lines pretty quickly, I can tell you. They hate to miss out on rehearsals.

The problem with actors learning an inflection as they learn the line is overcome by the fact that they are left with more time in rehearsal to try new things. In the traditional way of working, actors can be just as inflexible during the first performance, as they struggle to keep their memory ahead of the scene. It is only after the play has 'run itself in' for a couple of weeks that they are able to relax and listen and respond and become more instinctive in the way they use the text. But this creative freedom comes too late for the first-night audience.

So, although learning all the lines thoroughly before working on a scene may throw up a few problems, it has tremendous advantages. It gives the actors more time in rehearsal to *act* with each other. It gives them more time to be inventive. And it gives them more time to relax, communicate their objectives, listen and respond, and to be totally 'in the moment'.

Starting Work on a Scene

After a couple of weeks creating characters and exploring relationships through improvisation, learning lines and discussing emotions and objectives, it is now time to work on the text of the play. I usually divide the script up into bite-sized sections or scenes which have a sort of completeness about them. Whenever there is a change of subject, or a change of action, or a new character arrives, or someone leaves, I will make that the start of a new section. Each section usually turns out to be somewhere between three and seven minutes long. Enough for the actors to get their teeth into, but not so much that they are daunted by the magnitude of it.

The first thing I do when I'm working on a scene is to get the actors to run the lines. Some of them may have already found time to do this outside of rehearsals, but for most of them it will be the first time they have spoken the text in front of other people. I usually suggest that they wander around the room as they say their lines, without worrying where they should be onstage. Being on the move takes away some of the pressure and makes it easier for them to concentrate. I tell them they don't have to act, they just have to listen to the other actors and respond with their lines. They should also try to communicate the meaning or intention of their lines as they speak.

Playing the Intention, not the Emotion

If the actors are working on a particularly emotional scene I tell them that I don't want them to try to create the emotion at this stage of rehearsals. Instead, I ask them to think about the meaning of the words rather than the emotion behind them. I ask them to think about why their character is speaking. What their character wants when they speak. And what effect their character intends to have on other people when they say the lines.

I ask them to play the *intention*, not the *emotion*.

That phrase is like an acting mantra to me.

Briefly, the thinking goes like this: when someone speaks it's because they want to affect someone else. If they are angry with the other person and the line is 'Will you shut up?', then what they are trying to do is to stop the other person from talking. That is their *intention*. And that's what they need to express. If an actor is playing the *emotion* and not the intention, then they will just be screaming into the void – 'Will you shut up?!' – and the line loses its purpose. If they really want to shut the other person up, they have to start communicating their desire for the other person's silence by the way they speak. At this stage in rehearsals, the emotion can often blur the intention.

This is not to be confused with the way they *express* that intention. This can best be described in the form of a transitive verb, sometimes called the 'action'. The character's intention is to shut the other person up, but they can do it in a number of ways. They can *dominate* the other person as they say the line, they can *plead* with them, or they can *cajole* them, but whatever their 'action', their intention remains the same: to shut the other person up. For a more in-depth examination of 'actioning' and a full list of playable action verbs, see *Actions – The Actors Thesaurus* by Marina Caldarone and Maggie Lloyd-Williams (Nick Hern Books, 2004).

Sometimes, even at the beginning of rehearsals, the actors will have an idea of how the scene should ultimately sound, and they will want to try and make it happen as soon as possible. But they don't need to. If they 'push' too hard in the early stages, they will be playing the surface of an emotion and brushing over the subtle changing moods within the scene. There is plenty of time to develop a character's emotional state. So, to start with, let the words in the script tell them what their character wants and let them express that want, not the emotion behind it.

What's Been Happening?

Scenes start in all manner of ways: the lights could come up in the middle of a conversation; two people could walk onto the stage as if they had just walked into a room together; one person could have been in the room on their own and another could have just arrived; a crowd of courtiers could have been hanging around and the scene starts when the king enters. There are many variations. But the common link is that all the characters have been alive and have been doing something else before the action of a scene.

Often these previous activities will affect the characters' mood and, consequently, they will affect the way the characters behave, so I feel it's important for the actors to experience five or ten minutes of their character's life before the beginning of a scene.

And that can be done through improvisation.

Pre-scene Action

In discussion with the director and the rest of the cast, the actors should decide what their characters might have been doing before a scene starts. They could have been having tea and talking about the weather, or they could have been driving through the streets of London in a taxi, discussing the merits of marriage. The choice of scenario will be governed by the plot of the play and the opening dialogue. When everything has been decided, the actors can improvise the pre-scene action for about five to ten minutes and then let it flow into the first few lines of the text of the scene. For this first attempt, it is useful to give some indication of how the time is passing during this improvisation by letting the actors know when there are three minutes left until the start of the scene. Two minutes. One minute. And then thirty seconds. This gets everyone working to the same timescale.

Having improvised the pre-scene action once, there should be a discussion about the improvisation. Did it set the right tone for the actual scene? Were each character's emotions at the right level? Was the transition from improvisation to text smooth and believable? Did the improvised scene lead correctly into the mood and rhythm of the actual scene?

The School for Scandal by Richard Brinsley Sheridan

This eighteenth-century play starts with Lady Sneerwell and Snake in the middle of planning how to spread malicious gossip. They are in Lady Sneerwell's house, so the two actors could improvise a scene where Snake arrives and is shown in by a servant. Snake will be feeling pleased with himself because he has done everything that Lady Sneerwell has asked him to do, and Lady Sneerwell will want to get rid of the servant so she can hear the good news. Perhaps the servant could serve tea while Lady Sneerwell and Snake engage in polite conversation and wait for him to go. Perhaps Lady Sneerwell would be reading through something Snake has written and making comments about it, while Snake paces anxiously up and down. Whatever happens during the improvised scene will be underscored by anticipation and excitement, which could burst out when they start using the scripted dialogue. This would give the opening lines of the play an added energy and dynamism that might not have been there without this exploration.

Depending on what has happened during the improvisation, certain adjustments can be made in order to make the transition to text more organic. Maybe the servant in the example from *The School for Scandal* described above should have been a bit more stroppy. Maybe there should have been an increase in tension and mistrust between the characters. And so on.

Having had the discussion, the actors can improvise the pre-scene action for a second time in order to see what difference the adjustments make. It may be necessary to try this improvisation a third time, but usually a couple of versions at this stage will be enough to give the actors something to work with the next time they rehearse the text of the scene.

Entrances into a Scene

If a character enters a scene during the action, then the actor needs to have a clear idea of what their character has been doing in the minutes before they walk into the room. For instance, when Ernest/Jack Worthing arrives at Algernon's flat during the first scene of *The Importance of Being Earnest* by Oscar Wilde, how did he get there? Did he talk to anyone on the way? What did he say to the servant, Lane, who let him in? Did Lane take his coat? Are they friendly with each other?

When the five characters arrive at the restaurant one by one during the opening scene of *Top Girls* by Caryl Churchill, what have they experienced on the way there? Did one have a difficult journey? Did another sweep majestically through the streets? Did a third have to hurry because she was held up by traffic? Actually, this play is rather abstract, even metaphorical, and since these characters are all famous historical women one of them, Dull Gret, could have stepped out of a Brueghel painting or another, Lady Nijo, might have arrived directly from a thirteenth-century Japanese court. Wherever they were in their previous existence will influence their character's mood as they join the scene.

As with pre-scene action, any actor who is about to join a scene should have a discussion with the director and the other actors to decide what they think their character has been doing before they arrive. They could have come from another country, another part of town or from the house next door. Maybe they have come from another room in the house. Perhaps they were preparing dinner in the kitchen or playing cards with a bunch of friends in the dining room. They could arrive singly or in the middle of a conversation with someone else. Some of these things will be dictated by the script. If any other unscripted characters need to be involved – like a taxi driver, people in the street, a servant or a friend – then other members of the cast can take on these roles.

When an actor is involved in an improvisation and then has to arrive, on cue, during the scripted dialogue of a scene, it is quite difficult to get the timing right. What I tend to do is get the actors who are already in the scene to stand by while I concentrate on the new arrival's improvisation. When the new arrival seems to be ready to enter the scene, I signal for the other actors to start the final few lines of text before the new arrival's entrance. Once the entrance has happened, I usually let the scene continue for a page or two.

It sometimes goes a bit pear-shaped the first time that actors try this improvisation because everyone is concentrating on getting the timing right. So, after a discussion to iron out the problems, I usually get the actors to repeat the transition so the improvised action flows smoothly into the scripted text.

If a character needs a bit of help finding the right energy or emotion at the start of a scene, unexpected characters or events can be introduced by the director during subsequent improvisations. For instance, if a character is supposed to enter the scene feeling harassed and distracted, then another actor could play a police officer stopping them for questioning just before they arrive at the location of the scene. Or if a character is supposed to enter the sitting room feeling confident and relaxed, then another actor could pretend to be an old friend arriving for a cup of tea and chatting about the character's life in the kitchen.

This improvisation gives new arrivals to a scene a very clear sense of where they have come from and the mood they bring with them when they arrive, and that is useful for both the new arrival and the characters he or she joins mid-scene.

The Caretaker by Harold Pinter

The play starts with one character, Mick, alone in the room, but when he hears distant voices he gets up and leaves. There is silence. The voices are heard again getting nearer and nearer until eventually Aston and Davies enter the room. The dialogue starts when Aston says, 'Sit down.' Davies says, 'Thanks', looks around and sees that the only chair is lying on its side by the fireplace. As the scene progresses, we discover that Davies is a tramp who never stops talking and Aston is apparently rather slow-witted and doesn't say much at all.

What has happened before the scene starts is that Davies has been involved in a fight and has been kicked out of the place he was staying. Aston has stopped the fight, offered Davies a bed for the night and brought him home. So there has been a lot of physical and emotional action before the two characters walk into the room. The voices that Mick heard at the beginning of the scene must have been Davies rabbiting on as Aston let him into the house and led him up the stairs. This pre-entrance dialogue could be improvised to give the actors the right energy and level of emotion as they enter the room. But if the tension of the fight and Aston's rescue is missing, a second improvisation could include an argument and a bit of physical action (the actor playing Mick could help out as the other person in the fight) in order to give both of the actors the right level of adrenalin and physical exhaustion. It could also help Davies feel a sense of righteous indignation while giving Aston pride in the success of the rescue and confidence in his physical strength.

11

Developing a Scene

When I was at drama school a director called Peter Oyston came to teach us. This was a long time ago when the rehearsal process was quite different from how it is today. Most of the time the director would simply tell actors where to stand onstage so the audience could see their faces and that was about it. It was called 'blocking'. Terrible word. Think about it. Who wants to be blocked? In those days, actors learned their lines and their moves, and rehearsals were mainly about getting it all to run smoothly. Peter Oyston did things rather differently. He was a young Australian who looked a bit like Klaus Kinski in his intensity and he was hired to direct a second-year production of *Richard III*. This wasn't going to be shown to the public, so, as is often the case in drama schools, we divided up the main characters amongst several students. I got to play the first third of Richard: 'Now is the winter of our discontent…' etc.

How is it that some people come along and inspire you when you least expect it? Peter inspired me. He inspired lots of us. Students are a bit like that. We had loads of great teachers, but we all went mad for Peter. On one occasion he told us that the director should be a mirror for the actor to see his performance in. A great thought. Inspirational. And I truly believe it to this day.

At the beginning of rehearsals Peter got all three Richards together and said that the character was complicated enough and he didn't want us to spend loads of time worrying about a withered arm or a hunchback. He said that we should assume that the arm was an annoyance for Richard and he had decided to strap it up so it wouldn't get in the way. We thought that was a great idea, so we all brought belts to rehearsals and tied our right arms tightly to our bodies.

And that was how we rehearsed the play. We forgot about the withered arm and got on with trying to get the acting right.

Just before the one and only performance, Peter called all the Richards to one side, glared at us from under his blond fringe and said, 'Forget the belts.' 'What?' we said. 'Take off the belts,' he said. 'You don't need them.' We were shocked, but of course we were inspired, so we did what he said. When we performed the play, an amazing thing happened. We hadn't been able

to use our right arms for five weeks so we had been making all our gestures with our left hands. That was our Richard. That was what we did. So when it came to the performance, our right arms just hung limply at our sides without us thinking about them at all. Brilliant.

I had the opening speech of the play and it was a bit daunting. Richard's coat of arms has two boars holding up a shield, so Peter suggested that I used a boar as a way to explore the character. 'I want to see your boar!' he would shout at me. I had to start the play by walking from the back of the stage to the front, imagining that I was a boar coming over the brow of a hill and seeing my future mapped out before me. I loved it.

One day we were working on Richard's opening speech in a church hall in Swiss Cottage, and Peter said that I should say the speech imagining that Richard was massively excited about his future plans. Everyone was watching. I started and it began to feel good. That sometimes happens. When I got to the end of the speech I told him that his suggestion had really worked. Peter didn't seem interested. He just said, 'Do it again, but this time imagine that Richard is really angry about the way things have turned out.' I was a bit surprised, but I was willing to give it a go. 'OK,' I said.

This second time felt entirely different from the first, but the funny thing was, it still worked. After a few lines it had started to feel good.

When I finished I wanted to discuss the differences with Peter and ask him which he thought would be the best way to do it, but he still wasn't interested in talking about it. He just said, 'Do it again, but this time imagine that Richard is extremely sorry for himself and wants to cry.'

I tried it. It worked. What next?

'Try it again, but this time imagine that the boar is looking for a female boar and is only thinking of sex.'

We did about six versions of the speech, each one different and each one seemed to work.

With all the other students as an audience, Peter peered at me from under his fringe and said: 'Do you think you can do all six versions at the same time?'

WHAT?!

'I don't know,' I said, 'I'll give it a shot.'

I did. God knows how it turned out. It doesn't really matter. But that was when I realised that there was no single way to play a scene, there are just layers. Layers upon layers. Stop searching for a perfect version. Try everything and then try something more.

In case you're wondering what happened to Peter Oyston, he went back to Australia to run a drama school. Later in life he returned to England and I believe he is now a painter. I've never seen any of his paintings, but I bet they're imaginative and uncompromising. Perhaps it was the uncompromising nature of his rehearsals that inspired us. Perhaps it was the way he made us use our imaginations to build a character.

B Y USING ALL THE EXERCISES AND IMPROVISATIONS I HAVE described so far, the actors will have been gathering a great deal of knowledge and understanding. Enough to get by and enjoy themselves as actors exploring the alien landscape of a play. But in order to feel really connected to the play, in order to get the lifeblood of the play flowing through the veins of all the actors, there is still some work to be done. Further experiments. Deeper explorations. The director and the actors all need to feel as if they are living in the world of the play and not just visiting it.

Some of the improvisations in this chapter will enable the actors to gain a greater understanding of a scene while others will be, as it were, maintenance and repair. Problem-solving. Fine tuning. Servicing and road-testing. Taking a scene, which to all intents and purposes seems to be working, and making it work even better. Creating something which will give the audience a deeper understanding of the lives and actions of the characters, and at the same time clarify and illuminate the author's intentions.

Improvising a Scene in Your Own Words

A common and very productive rehearsal tool is to ask the actors to improvise the scene in their own words. This is particularly useful if you're working on a text that has a complex language structure like a Shakespeare play or a Greek tragedy, because it helps the actors think about what their characters are actually trying to say to each other, rather than worrying about the intricate, heightened language that they are using.

For instance, when Romeo and Juliet first meet, they have the most complicated piece of dialogue that you can possibly imagine. Not only is the language difficult and the images hard to follow, but the first fourteen lines they speak to each other are, in fact, a sonnet. They share it. Romeo has the first four lines and Juliet the next four. Then they have a line each. Romeo has the next two before they finish it off, again with a line each. Then they kiss. How romantic.

Shakespeare was famous for his sonnets but this is the only time he used one as part of the dialogue in a play. Sonnets are often love poems and this is the greatest love story of all time. The prologue of *Romeo and Juliet* is also a sonnet: 'Two households, both alike in dignity…' etc. Talk about getting everyone in the right mood.

But to get back to the dialogue between Romeo and Juliet: not only is it a poem, with a complicated pattern of rhymes, the actual images are also hard to fathom. For a start, the name 'Romeo' is another word for pilgrim. As is the word 'palmer'. Juliet makes a pun out of this when she says that pilgrims put their hands together 'palm to palm' as in prayer. But Romeo has suggested that Juliet's hand is a shrine and that Juliet is the saint he has come to worship, so he says that pilgrims use their lips for prayer and, therefore, he and Juliet should put their lips together instead of their hands. Juliet says that if she is a saint she shouldn't make the first move but she should grant him his wish (answer his prayer). He tells her to stand still so he can kiss her. Which she does. And he kisses her.

If you find that hard to understand, try reading the actual text:

ROMEO.   If I profane with my unworthiest hand
              This holy shrine, the gentle sin is this;
              My lips, two blushing pilgrims, ready stand
              To smooth that rough touch with a tender kiss.

JULIET.   Good pilgrim, you do wrong your hand too much,
              Which mannerly devotion shows in this;
              For saints have hands that pilgrims' hands do touch,
              And palm to palm is holy palmers' kiss.

ROMEO.   Have not saints lips, and holy palmers too?

JULIET.   Ay, pilgrim, lips that they must use in prayer.

ROMEO.   O! then, dear saint, let lips do what hands do;
              They pray, grant thou, lest faith turn to despair.

JULIET.   Saints do not move, though grant for prayers' sake.

ROMEO.   Then move not, while my prayers' effect I take.
              He kisses her.

Having worked out the meaning of this rhetoric, the actors then have to see if they can make the images clear for the audience. The trouble is that when they do that, they can lose sight of the feelings of love and romance that their characters are supposed to feel for each other. In a case like this, an improvisation using their own words will free the actors from the complexities of the text and allow them to imagine that they are teenagers falling in love for the first time, and subsequently rediscover the emotion of the scene.

In this particular instance I would work on the scene through a series of improvisations in order to help the actors come to terms with the way that Romeo and Juliet are able to use complex rhetorical devices in their everyday speech.

Two People Falling in Love

First of all, the actors should improvise a modern scene in their own words where two young people fall in love at first sight.

Using a Modern Metaphor

Then I would ask them to think of a modern metaphor that they themselves might use about love. For instance, 'Romantic thoughts flying like text messages.' Then, still using their own words, I would ask them to improvise the scene again using this modern metaphor to see if they can be inventive and clever, and still retain a sense of romance and emotion. Maybe the improvisation would go something like this:

ROMEO. I've been hoping to meet someone like you.

JULIET. What's the point of hoping if no one knows about it?

ROMEO. All my friends on Facebook know how desperate I am.

JULIET. Then you'll have to ask me to be your friend or I'd never get the message.

ROMEO. Will you be my friend?

JULIET. Yes, if you text me your address.

ROMEO. My message will fly through the network on wings of love.

JULIET. Careful it doesn't get lost in cyberspace.

ROMEO. I want to be lost in your arms.

JULIET. Then log onto Hotmail before you cool off.

(I want to make a pun about Romeo being a 'hot male', but that would be just too tacky. Even for Shakespeare.)

Modernising Shakespeare's Metaphor

Having done that, I would ask the pair to improvise the scene for a third time, still using their own words but this time using the same metaphor that Shakespeare uses. They shouldn't try to modernise the scene line by line, but they should use the metaphor of Juliet being a shrine and Romeo being a pilgrim quite broadly and loosely, whilst still trying to retain the emotion and truth of the meeting.

It may stray wildly from the structure of Shakespeare's dialogue, but it will give the actors a sense of how their characters might enjoy using metaphors. Maybe the improvised dialogue would go something like this:

ROMEO. I've never met anyone like you.

JULIET. There's millions of girls like me. You can't have looked far.

ROMEO. I took a year out to travel round the world.

JULIET. What for?

ROMEO. To find myself.

JULIET. And did you?

ROMEO. I've found you. My trip has been a pilgrimage and now I'm in the holy land.

JULIET. Welcome, pilgrim.

ROMEO. And you are the holy shrine. I want to worship you.

JULIET. If I'm a shrine, then you must go on your knees and pray to me.

ROMEO. I'd rather kiss you.

JULIET. It's true, pilgrims often kiss a holy statue, but that's religious devotion rather than lust.

ROMEO. But I'm devoted to you.

JULIET. Then show your devotion by praying to me. Pray that your wishes will come true and I might consent.

ROMEO. Then I pray that we can kiss each other.

JULIET. Gods listen to prayers but they don't always make them come true. Sometimes the worshipper has to put a bit more effort into getting what he wants.

ROMEO. All right. If you let me kiss you, I will love you for ever.

JULIET. Go on then, but remember: gods don't always kiss back.

ROMEO. They do if pilgrims are honest and true.

JULIET. Are you?

ROMEO. I'm mad about you.

JULIET. You're mad all right. The mad pilgrim.

ROMEO. And if we kiss, my prayers will come true.

JULIET. Go on then, pilgrim, kiss the shrine.

ROMEO. All right. If you want me to, I will.

JULIET. I do.

Not nearly as clever as Shakespeare, but that's not the point. As the actors play around with the metaphor, they will understand how Romeo and Juliet feel when they are playing around with the metaphor that Shakespeare has written for them.

Using Shakespeare's Text

Finally, I would ask the actors to play the scene as written, but still try to retain the sense of creative enjoyment and spontaneity that they have discovered during the improvisations.

Improvising the Subtext

Subtext can be a minefield. If mishandled it can lead to ridiculously overplayed inner emotions. Strange really, since the whole purpose of subtext is for the actor to understand what their characters really feel, or what they really think, as they speak the dialogue. The characters in Chekhov's plays, for instance, are full of unstated emotions and desires. They talk about the weather or the theatre or cherry orchards. They discuss going to Moscow, or the destruction of rural life. They drink, play music and they eat. But underneath all this, they are seething with inexpressible passion. They are hopelessly in love. They are suicidally depressed. They are green with jealousy, they are bored and they are angry. But they don't talk about these things. They can't!

So when Yelena asks if she can have Astrov's pencil in *Uncle Vanya*, what she is really asking for is Astrov himself. She is desperate, but she knows she can't have him, and two minutes later they say goodbye for ever. Admittedly, she grabs a parting kiss, but she knows it's the end of a relationship they never really had. The kiss symbolises something that was never going to be and the pencil is the only part of him that she can keep.

When actors are playing a scene like that, they need to understand what is going on deep down in their character's soul. Of course they do. They need to know the subtext. It must flow through them like their lifeblood. But they mustn't perform the subtext. They must keep it hidden. What they must perform is the text itself, as written. When Yelena asks for the pencil, she must simply ask for the pencil. That's what she wants. Often people in real life are trying to hide what they are really thinking and wanting, and that's what actors must do. The more subtle and delicate the actress playing Yelena makes her subtextual desire for Astrov, the more the audience will be moved by the hopelessness of her situation. Subtext must be 'sub'. It mustn't be demonstrated; otherwise it just becomes a new 'text'.

However, an exploration of the subtext will give the actors a greater understanding of what they are trying to hide. These emotions and thoughts hidden beneath the surface of the dialogue can be improvised in a number of ways.

⚡ Vocalising the Subtext

This is an exercise that most of us are familiar with because we've seen it used in films and comedy sketches. Woody Allen uses it brilliantly in his film Annie Hall. It's when you hear a voice-over or see subtitles of the characters thoughts after each phrase of spoken dialogue:

'You look great.' (Voice-over: 'My God, she's aged.')

'So do you.' (Voice-over: 'Bitch! She knows I've gone grey.')

'Where did you get that dress?' (Voice-over: 'From a charity shop?')

'Oh, this old thing?' (Voice-over: 'It cost me £250!')

You know the thing. People love it because they recognise it as something that happens all the time. Social conventions cover a multitude of perilous thoughts.

This technique can be used when actors are rehearsing a scene. Simply ask them to improvise their subtextual thoughts out loud after they have spoken each line of the text. Of course, the scene will unfold slowly, but the results will be extremely revealing for the actors.

⚡ Playing the Subtext

This improvisation takes the previous exercise one step further. Rather than saying the scripted lines, you ask the actors to speak just the subtext of the scene. There are several versions of this:

• The actors can abandon the shape and structure of the scene altogether and just play the underlying subtext, the hidden emotional life of the characters. In the case of the scene from Uncle Vanya, Yelena would fling her arms around Astrov and say, 'I love you and I want us to be together. Let's run away…', because that is what she really wants. This improvisation allows the actors to express openly the hidden emotions of their characters.

• As above, the actors can play the underlying subtext, but this time they should let it be tempered by the circumstances of the scene. In the case of Yelena, she would say something like, 'You know I love you and I want us to be together, but I also know it can never happen...' These are her thoughts at the moment that Astrov is about to leave. This improvisation will give the actors a sense of what is happening beneath the surface of the actual scene.

- If the actors know the text well enough, they play the whole scene speaking the subtext of each line without actually saying the line. It's probably helpful to practise vocalising the subtext first, so the actors are familiar with the way the scene unfolds. In this example, when Yelena asks for Astrov's pencil, rather than saying, 'I'm taking this pencil as a keepsake', she would say something like, 'Give me your pencil so I can keep my memory of you alive for the rest of my life.' This improvisation clarifies the subtle changes going on in the characters' hidden feelings and emotions.

Physicalising the Subtext

Having experimented with improvising the subtext, the actors can then be asked to play the scene using the text as written, but they should 'think' the subtext as they say the lines, and act it out physically. When Yelena asks for Astrov's pencil, her eyes would be yearning with love, and her clenched fists and raised shoulders could physicalise her inner torment. And although this may become physically mannered and unnaturalistic, it doesn't matter because it allows the actors to release and explore their character's inner thoughts at the same time as they speak their lines.

Thinking the Subtext

Finally, the actors should play the scene using the text as written and thinking about the subtext as they say each line. As they do this, they should try to keep the subtext hidden. This gets them closer to the way that people actually behave in reality.

The Dynamics of a Scene

When Peter Brook was directing his famous production of *A Midsummer Night's Dream* for the Royal Shakespeare Company in the early seventies (it was so famous it was known simply as 'Brook's Dream') he reportedly set up an improvisation which was a perfect example of improvising the dynamics of a scene.

Most people know *A Midsummer Night's Dream*, but briefly, part of the plot concerns a group of local artisans, known as the 'rude mechanicals', who are rehearsing a play for Duke Theseus and his friends. Eventually these mechanicals perform their play for the court. It's a very funny scene with the Duke and his friends interrupting all the time and the mechanicals being very nervous and getting things wrong. This is the first time in the play that the mechanicals and the members of the court get to meet.

Apparently, Peter Brook rehearsed the two groups of actors quite separately during the first part of the rehearsal process. They didn't even meet. The mechanicals rehearsed their scenes and the performance of their play without the interruptions from the court, and the people in the court didn't rehearse this final scene at all.

One day Brook told the actors playing the Duke and his court that they were going to improvise a party. He brought in some wine and food and loads of random costumes and told them to dress up in any way they liked and have fun. Unbeknownst to these actors, the actors playing the mechanicals had been asked to dress in their best suits and come to the rehearsal prepared to perform their play. When the court's party was in full swing, the mechanicals suddenly appeared and started their performance. The actors playing the Duke and his court were a bit drunk, and in a riotous mood, but of course, they soon twigged what was happening and started to make fun of the mechanicals. The actors playing the mechanicals must have been completely thrown off-kilter as they nervously tried to perform their play for the first time. Perhaps they forgot their lines. Perhaps they tried all sorts of ways to hold the attention of the courtiers. The courtiers, on the other hand, started to have fun and enjoy their invulnerable high status. I wasn't at the rehearsals but I was lucky enough to see the show, and like everything else in this magical production, the scene was brilliantly conceived and performed.

Improvising the Dynamics

When I was directing *A View from the Bridge* by Arthur Miller, one of the scenes wasn't working very well. It's quite a dynamic moment in the play when a couple of immigration officers burst into an apartment, arrest some illegal immigrants and take them off down the street. When we rehearsed the scene the people in the apartment didn't seem to be shocked or frightened by the incident, and the immigration officers found it all too easy to make the arrest. Not every immigrant in the apartment was illegal, but the immigration officers seemed to know exactly which people to arrest and where they were hiding, despite never having seen them before. This was obviously because they knew which actor was playing which part.

For the next rehearsal I told the immigration officers to go and work on their characters in another room while I worked with the immigrants. I had an improvisation in mind but, like Peter Brook, I didn't tell anyone what I was going to ask them to do.

There is a scene in the play where a few of the immigrants have a little party, so once the immigration officers had left the room, I asked the rest of the actors to play immigrants and improvise a party. I told them that they shouldn't be their characters in the play but they had to decide who among them were going to be legal immigrants and who were going to be illegal. I put on some appropriate music and let the improvisation begin.

Once the party was in full swing I left the room to speak to the immigration officers. I told them that the rest of the group were improvising an immigrants' party in the other room but that none of the other actors were playing their actual characters.

The immigration officers had to burst in, decide who were the illegal immigrants, and arrest them.

It was chaos. The music was very loud. The immigration officers had to shout to be heard. Some people didn't take any notice of them. Some of the immigrants started covering up for each other. Some of them started to lie outrageously. Some of them tried to keep a low profile. There were lots of misunderstandings and arguments, and the immigration officers had to become quite violent and aggressive to get anyone's attention. Eventually they arrested several people and took them away. Funnily enough, they didn't arrest entirely the right people.

We then rehearsed the scene as it was written, using the scripted lines. But in addition to this, I also asked everyone to improvise dialogue in any way they wanted. There were two immigration officers, four legal immigrants and six illegal immigrants in the room and when they were taken out into the street, there were about eight more nosy neighbours who had created characters using the crowd scene improvisation described below.

When the actors ran the scene, the atmosphere was as shocking and as dynamic as you could wish because the actors had *experienced* the incident and consequently knew how to play it. No one was given any moves that they had to stick to and every time we rehearsed or performed the scene, the actors were free to do or say what they liked, providing they also used the text as it was written. The scene was dynamic and dangerous in every performance because no one knew exactly what to expect.

Improvising a Crowd Scene

I can't stand it when you go to the theatre and see the actors who are playing the crowd standing around like stuffed dummies trying not to steal the audience's focus. It's even worse when they have been directed to react on a certain line and they shout out on cue and then shut up again. It's all so phoney.

I think this 'stealing focus' malarkey is a bit of a myth. Stuffed dummies steal the focus far more than real-life people reacting truthfully. And anyway, sometimes it's great to have the focus spinning around the stage from person to person. It's exciting to watch. The actors with the lines can grab hold of the focus whenever they want. They've got the plot in their hands. Let everyone else bring *life* to the stage. That's what theatre is all about.

Of course, you can't create the proper dynamics if the actors in the crowd don't know who they are, where they are and what they want. In order to make a crowd scene work, the actors have to create proper characters, develop relationships with other characters and do the same sort of research into the environment of the play as the rest of the cast. They need to be fully conversant with the 'world' of the play: the politics of the period, the social conventions, the climate of the times, etc., etc.

Next, they should each create a believable character. This should be fun because they can be anyone they like within the conventions of the play. Using the work described in Chapter 4: Preparing a Character, all the people in the crowd should create truthful and realistic characters.

Then they should invent relationships amongst themselves. Two people could decide to be a husband and wife, for instance. Two others could decide that they hate each other because one of them cheated the other out of money a few years ago. A small group could be workmates or have been friends since school. Anything they like. If the actors are familiar with this way of working, it will only take them a few minutes to talk about relationships and make some decisions. They can then do a couple of improvisations and after about half an hour they'll have a workable sense of who they are and what they feel about each other.

Next, they should decide why their characters are at the location of the scene and what they want. This will vary for every play but broadly speaking there are two options. One is that they are there because they are part of the plot and have come to see what's going on; the other is that they just happen to be there and they get involved, to a greater or lesser extent, just by chance. If it's the latter version, it's important that they know why they have come to that particular location. Maybe they are going shopping with a friend. Maybe they want to meet someone in the town square. Maybe two of them are having a romantic stroll together so they can make wedding plans. These details give the actors something to act.

Having done that work, you can set up a group improvisation in the location of the scene, but without the scene actually taking place. For instance, if you were rehearsing the scene in *Julius Caesar* where Mark Antony speaks to the citizens over Caesar's dead body ('Friends, Romans, countrymen, lend me your ears…'), you can ask the crowd to improvise a normal day at the forum, without Mark Antony, without the dead Caesar, without any drama, in order to let them focus on their characters, their relationships and their reason to be there in the first place. After they've been improvising this scene for ten or fifteen minutes, it would be useful to ask one of the other actors to address the crowd about a tax increase, or a change in the political structure, so the group can find out how they might respond to some sort of high-status orator.

If the actors playing the named characters and speaking the text have learned their lines thoroughly, you can now bring them into the scene and rehearse it with the improvising citizens. As the scene progresses, the actors in the crowd should be allowed to do anything they like, as long as they remain truthful to the plot and the situation. They can move where they want and they can say anything they like. Each actor should feel that their character *as a person* is just as important as any of the other characters in the scene. The actors in the crowd should only be 'respectful' to the actors with lines if their *characters* would be respectful towards them.

It's important to tell the actors with text that it doesn't matter if their lines are drowned out by the improvising citizens. This is a rehearsal exploration. It's better to allow the crowd to be creative in order to establish a dynamic interaction. Adjustments can be made later.

Generally speaking, I have found that, rather than having to tame an ultra-noisy crowd that is continually getting in the way, I have to encourage the actors to be inventive and bold, because their theatrical instinct is to avoid 'stealing focus'. But the funny thing is, that when everyone in the crowd is active and alive, they don't steal focus. They homogenise. The audience tends not to notice them. Probably because the plot of the play is more interesting than the individual improvised reactions. And it's wonderful to see an actor having to fight to be heard in the same way that Mark Antony would have to fight to be heard in front of the real citizens:

'Friends, Romans, countrymen, lend me your ears.'

And how! They'll only listen if you make 'em, mate!

The crowd has to respond truthfully during a scene, just like any other actor. Sometimes there is a tendency to 'block' a natural response because the actors in the crowd become so involved in their imaginative creations. But, as I said, adjustments can always be made later in rehearsals. For me, the important thing is for the actors playing the crowd not to feel inhibited. They can be trusted. They are creative people too, and they can bring life, dynamism and excitement to a scene if they are allowed to.

⚡ Improvising the Objectives

Scenes unfold and develop in the way that playwrights want them to, not necessarily the way the characters they have created would like them to go. If they did, you often wouldn't get a play at all. Imagine if Claudius had been successful in his plan to kill Hamlet by giving Laertes a secretly poisoned sword so that everyone would think that Hamlet's death was the result of a fencing accident. There would have been a lot of sadness in the court, but Laertes, Claudius and Gertrude would still be alive. Claudius would carry on ruling Denmark, and Fortinbras would have had to continue his rampage around Northern Europe instead of becoming the next king. What if Friar Lawrence's ridiculous plan had worked? Juliet would have woken up from her drug-induced, death-like sleep in plenty of time to live happily ever after with her new husband Romeo.

Plots are often constructed around plans going wrong.

There is a rather tricky, but fabulous, scene in Oscar Wilde's *The Importance of Being Earnest* when Gwendolen and Cecily meet for the first time. It's a very complicated plot. But briefly:

- Gwendolen is engaged to be married to Jack, but thinks his name is Ernest.

- Jack is the guardian of his beautiful young niece and ward Cecily who lives in Jack's country house.

- Jack's friend Algernon goes to the country to see Cecily, but he pretends to be Jack's brother Ernest. Cecily instantly falls in love with him and they get engaged to be married.

- Gwendolen decides to check out Jack's country house (where Cecily lives) while he is away.

- When Gwendolen arrives at Jack's country house and meets Cecily, they discover that they are both engaged to be married to a person called Ernest. (In fact, neither of them are.) Great confusion. Brilliant scene.

What happens during the scene is that the two girls start off by being very nice and polite to each other, but then, as the scene unfolds, they start to hate each other and have a sort of battle of words and manners. Their language is sometimes quite insulting and I have seen the scene played with both the girls being quite nasty to each other, spitting venom as they verbally scratched each other's eyes out. But I think that way of playing the scene misses the point. The scene is a pastiche of the false etiquette and manners of the time, and I think that Oscar Wilde's intention was that the girls should be trying desperately to be refined and polite as they hurl their masked insults.

This is a perfect example of how improvisation can be used to explore what the characters actually want, by isolating various objectives. If the actresses have improvised the scene unfolding in the way their character would have *liked* it to go, then they will be able to understand how their objectives are thwarted, and as a result it will reveal the pattern of their shifting emotions. Here's what I suggest:

- An improvisation where Gwendolen meets the sort of Cecily that she would have hoped was Jack's ward: 'fully forty-two, and more than usually plain for (her) age.' (An older actress could take on this role.) Hopefully the scene would be polite, refined and rather boring.

- An improvisation where Cecily meets a stranger from London who she is able to charm and flatter. Hopefully the actress playing the immature Cecily would be able to explore her attempt at some sort of sophistication.

- An improvisation where Gwendolen and Cecily meet for the first time, but there is no mention of their engagements or of Ernest. Hopefully this version would be a bonding experience for the two young girls and they would become 'great friends' and 'like each other more than they can say', as they initially seem to do in Wilde's scene.

- An improvisation where the misunderstanding about Gwendolen and Cecily's engagements to Ernest takes place and they are allowed to express their hatred and mistrust of each other without adhering to the social restraints of the time. In this way they could unleash their emotions at full throttle rather than trying to mask them.

Having explored these alternative versions of the scene, the actors would be able to refer back to them when they come to play the text. They would have a clearer understanding of how their characters are feeling and what they are trying to cover up, and consequently the scene would develop a more complex web of changing moods and emotions. In the later section on improvising using the text, I will show how the actors can use the conventions and etiquette of the time to disguise these emotions while allowing the subtext to be subtly and insultingly revealed.

Improvising the Essence of a Scene

Sometimes the characters in a scene appear to be doing one thing, but in actual fact they are doing something else. There's a scene in the film *The Thomas Crown Affair* where Steve McQueen and Faye Dunaway are, to all intents and purposes, playing a game of chess. The reason the scene is so well known is because each chess move symbolises the seductive games that men and women play when they fancy each other. The chess game starts with Steve making a confident opening move. Faye responds immediately. No hanging around. They are both up for it. He responds with his knight, a symbol of strength in battle, and she counters with what appears to be her knight. (It's half out of shot.) They smile at each other. Equals. They play a few more moves. Steve grins with confidence as he appears to take control of the game. Faye smiles at him, humouring his naivety, and takes one of his pieces. Steve looks worried and confused. Nervous. He's losing confidence. She distracts him by leaning forward and exposing a little more of her cleavage. He tries to concentrate, wondering what to do next. He makes an uncertain move and she confidently begins to take control of the game. They size each other up. Has she been too dominating? She makes a bold move. Checkmate. He thinks for a moment, abandons the game and takes her in his arms and suggests that they play a different sort of game. She's fine about that. They are on the same wavelength. The scene is about a game of chess, but the underlying 'essence' of the scene is seduction.

It's quite probable that neither Steve McQueen nor Faye Dunaway needed any lessons in the art of seduction, but there are cases where the underlying essence of a scene is outside the actors' experience.

The hostages in *Someone Who'll Watch Over Me* by Frank McGuinness are locked in a cell, and they continually fantasise and play games with each other. These games often take the form of role-playing and are used to ease the frustration of imprisonment. For instance, when one hostage first arrives in the cell, another hostage bullies him as if the new arrival is a new boy in a posh public school. At the same time, the new arrival, who is totally confused, behaves as if he is in a madhouse. When I was rehearsing the play, none of the cast had been to a posh school, nor had they been inmates in a mental asylum, so I set up a couple of improvisations where they acted out these things. They had to maintain the spirit of their characters, but pretend that they were schoolboys in order to find out how their characters might behave if they really were at public school. They then played another improvisation where the two existing hostages could behave as if they were completely mad, in order for the new arrival to find out what it might be like to be thrust among lunatics.

In another scene the three hostages are pretending to get drunk and have a party, so I set up an improvisation where they had to pretend that their characters were at an actual beach party on a Greek island. In that way, they could explore the essence of the scene without also having to imagine they were locked in a cell in Lebanon, fearing for their lives.

In another section of the play, two of the hostages behave like children and pretend they are soaring over Europe in a flying car, Chitty Chitty Bang Bang. So I asked them to improvise a scene as if they really were children, in order to discover how their characters might play together. The scene shows how the hostages would use their imagination to escape from their terrible ordeal, but the essence of the scene is children at play. So I let them explore that.

The final scene is an interesting one, because by this time there are only two hostages left in the cell. One is about to be released and the other will have to continue as a hostage on his own. The scene appears to be about saying goodbye and trying to express their feelings for one another, but the underlying essence of the scene is confusion and uncertainty because neither of them know what will happen next. This time I got them to use the text as it is written (see *Improvising Using the Text*, below), but I told them that I was going to give each of them some secret information before they started. First of all, I whispered in the departing hostage's ear that he was convinced that he was going to be executed rather than be released but he didn't want to say anything about it because he knew it would upset the other hostage. I then whispered to the hostage remaining imprisoned that he was convinced that the other was going to be executed rather than be released but he didn't want to say anything about it because he knew it would upset him. In other words, they both thought that the released hostage was going to be executed, but neither of them thought the other knew. With the underlying essence of uncertainty and dread, the improvisation took on the right sort of tension and the actors were able to use this discovery when they next performed the scene.

⚡ Improvising Using the Text

This sounds like a contradiction in terms (and if you think improvisation just means making up the words as you go along, then it is). But it's also possible to use the text and improvise the *dynamics* of a scene by isolating and emphasising various aspects of the subtext.

The scene between Gwendolen and Cecily from *The Importance of Being Earnest* would be perfect for this kind of improvisation because there are a number of repressed dynamics woven throughout the scene as it unfolds. For instance, it would be very beneficial for the actresses to play the dialogue as if Gwendolen and Cecily really did like each other and their complements were heartfelt. They would possibly uncover a disappointed sense of sorrow as they started to dislike each other.

To explore another dynamic, the two actresses could play the scene again and really let fly with their bitchiness and hatred in order to unleash the inner feelings of their characters.

A third version could be one that is entirely governed by manners and social graces. Everything could be contained, polite and apparently generous of spirit.

After these improvisations, the two actresses would be able to play the scene combining all the elements because that is what the scene demands. When Gwendolen says at the beginning of the scene, 'Something tells me that we are going to be great friends', she really means it. When she later says, 'You are presumptuous. On an occasion of this kind it becomes more than a moral duty to speak one's mind. It becomes a pleasure', she is outraged and means to hurt Cecily's feelings. Yet within a few lines she is able to use all her social graces and best manners to ask, 'Are there many interesting walks in the vicinity, Miss Cardew?' What makes the scene interesting is the struggle that both characters have, particularly Gwendolen, to maintain the calm equilibrium that etiquette demands, while, at the same time, balancing and repressing their shifting emotions. This is where the humour lies. Oscar Wilde's intention was to satirise the affected manners and phoney etiquette of the age.

⚡ Blending Improvised and Scripted Dialogue

Another way to improvise but still use the text is when improvised dialogue is blended with the scripted text. I've already given an example of this when I described the immigration officers arresting illegal immigrants in *A View from the Bridge*. The actors without text – some of the illegal immigrants and the onlookers in the street – improvised their own dialogue while the actors using the text played the scene. This only works if everyone has a full understanding of what the play is trying to achieve; what story the playwright wants to tell.

The main danger with this kind of work is that people tend to mumble the improvised dialogue because they are afraid of spoiling the scene. Scripted dialogue and improvised dialogue must be given equal weight, otherwise it sounds phoney. Providing the director keeps an eye on the scene and makes the right adjustments, and all the actors focus on the function of the scene, the actors with text will always be heard.

A few years ago I was working on *Ah! Wilderness* by Eugene O'Neill. This play is about an ordinary middle-class American family at the beginning of the twentieth century. One scene takes place at a family dinner with the husband and wife, their four children, a maiden aunt and a family friend. Eight people in total. As written, the scene is beautifully crafted with the dialogue moving to various parts of the table so the audience can follow the interweaving plot lines. However, in the nature of the play it seemed unnatural that the younger children would be quiet all the time until it was their turn for a line of dialogue.

First of all, we improvised the scene without using the written text at all. The actors were able to create a very lively improvised dinner scene which was true to their characters and kept close to the storyline. I then asked everyone to use the text, but when they weren't speaking they were free to make up any lines they wanted. It was chaos. The scene was lively all right, but it was obviously difficult to remember the text when your 'children' were shouting for more potatoes and fighting amongst themselves. We persevered. Each time we rehearsed the scene, the actors became more and more confident with the text, so they could, for instance, say a line of scripted dialogue, turn to give an improvised answer to an improvised question, and turn back to continue with the text. It became organic. What made it more exciting was that the improvised dialogue was different every time we ran the scene, so no one knew exactly what to expect. It sounds like uncontrollable mayhem, but I was working with actors who were very experienced in this type of work and they knew how to keep the shifting focus of the scene intact as they made their unscripted contributions. The audience probably thought it was all very carefully planned and rehearsed, but in fact, each performance was entirely different. I'll never forget the way that Ali Playford – the mother – handled her unruly improvising family, improvising answers to their demands, ladling out the food, and never missing a beat of the script. It was a delight, it was exciting and it was full of life.

Problem-solving

So, having created characters, developed relationships, isolated and explored the essence of a scene and empowered the crowd, what else is there to be done? Well, each director has his or her own methods of rehearsing, clarifying, refining and perfecting a play until it becomes an illustration of their particular theatrical values and beliefs, and I wouldn't want to interfere. But there is still more improvising that can be done if things aren't going right. Perhaps one of the actors is uncertain about their work; maybe the inner life of one of the characters isn't clear or isn't even properly understood; perhaps one of the scenes has the wrong dynamics; maybe the cast doesn't understand the director's particular vision. At any time an unexpected difficulty can raise its ugly head. There are thousands of pitfalls and problems that can be experienced during the period of rehearsal. That's what makes it fun. I've yet to meet anyone who has a foolproof formula for theatrical success, and if I do I would advise them to look for another job. One that is more exciting, creative and fulfilling for them. Overcoming problems is one of the things that stimulates creativity. A crisis will always invigorate a stumbling imagination. I'm surprised that artists have any hair left to tear out.

However, I'm afraid you're going to have to invent your own problem-solving improvisations. I couldn't possibly try to guess all the difficulties that could arise during the rehearsal period of a play. All I can do, and hope I've done in this book, is open your mind to the possibilities of improvisation as a rehearsal tool, because I believe it can be a great way of resolving problems. As I've said before, actors love to immerse themselves in their own imagination and use it for exploration and discovery, and improvisation is a full-on, one-hundred-per-cent leap into the creative imagination of an actor. Let them resolve a crisis by *doing* something about it. Actors can act. Allow them to use their unique gifts and talents to cut deep to the heart of a rehearsal problem. They have an instinctive knowledge of human behaviour and improvisation gives them the opportunity to exploit that knowledge.

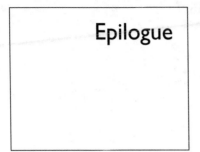

Epilogue

THE INTENTION OF THIS BOOK IS TO DESCRIBE A VARIETY of ways in which improvisation can be used during the rehearsals of a play. However, it's important to stress that this sort of improvisation is not an end in itself. It should only be used to help the actors during the creative process and to support and illuminate the intentions of the writer. Too often, people can get carried away by marvellous rehearsal explorations that make them feel extremely creative but in fact don't benefit the play at all. Let me stress that there is no point in doing this sort of work if it doesn't clarify the text or if it doesn't give the audience a better understanding of the characters and their actions. The purpose of rehearsals is to enrich and refine a play; it is not to use the text as a springboard for creating a new play. If you want to do that, then write your own! Or improvise one from scratch.

But for now:

THE PLAY'S THE THING.

And improvisation can be used to create a wonderful and comprehensive version of the play by using actors to explore the subtleties and nuances of the writer's handiwork. It will enable the actors to tell the story in a way that moves, excites and thrills an audience. And what could be better than that?

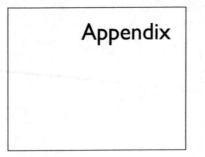

Appendix

This appendix provides a quick reminder of all the exercises and improvisations described in the book. In some cases I have indicated, in square brackets, the amount of time I would allow for each exercise or improvisation.

Chapter 1 – Preparation (*page 15*)

Before any practical work on a play, the actors should gather as much information as possible.

Looking for Clues (*page 17*)

The actors should read the play several times and make a note of all the facts they discover in the text.

They should take notes about the given circumstances of the play; i.e. the time of year, the location, the interior décor, etc.

They should take notes of all the information in the text about their character; i.e. 'I'm so bored', 'I usually take the bus to work', etc.

They should take notes of all the opinions their character has of other people, their surroundings and the world in general.

First Reading (*page 19*)

The whole cast should read the play, stopping for a discussion after each scene or section.

After reading the play, the cast should have a longer discussion.

Character Discussions (*page 20*)

In groups of four or five, the cast should discuss everything they know about each character in the group. Each group should be made up of characters who would know something about each other; i.e. family members, long-term friends, etc. [*15 mins per character*].

Relationship Discussions (*page 21*)

The actors whose characters have a relationship in the play should get together to discuss that relationship [*15 mins per relationship*].

The Social and Physical Environment of the Play (*page 23*)

The whole cast should discuss anything they have discovered in the text about the world of the play.

Chapter 2 – Research (*page 27*)

With a large cast, research can be done in small groups with each group feeding back their research to the rest of the cast [*20 mins for each feedback subject*]. At the same time everyone should be trying to find any visual material that may be of help. Subjects for research:

The Playwright (*page 30*)

One group can research the playwright's biography and to read other plays he or she has written.

Transport, Furniture and Fashion (*page 33*)

One group can research the modes of travel, furniture and clothing of the period and/or place in which the production is set.

Codes of Conduct and Acceptable Behaviour (*page 36*)

One group can research the social customs and acceptable etiquette of the period and/or place in which the production is set.

Political Climate (*page 38*)

One group can research the political climate of the period and/or place in which the production is set.

Thematic Research (*page 39*)

One group can research the various themes or topics in the play.

Chapter 3 – Background Improvisations (*page 42*)

In order to give the cast shared background knowledge, the actors can try the following group improvisations as themselves, not as their characters in the play.

Street-life Exercise (*page 46*)

Using the research information gathered so far, the actors should imagine they are walking alone down a street, a path or a road from the period and/or place in which the production is set [*15 mins*].

Street-life Improvisation (*page 46*)

With the whole cast working together as a group, but not using their characters from the play, the actors should give themselves suitable roles and relationships. They can then improvise the street-life (or any communal open-air area) from the period and/or place in which the production is set [*15 mins*].

Street-life Improvisations in Character (*page 47*)

Once the actors have a clear idea of their characters and their relationships with other characters, the actors can do the above improvisation as their characters in the play [*20 mins*].

Social Dance Improvisation (*page 50*)

With the whole cast working together as a group, but not using their characters from the play, the actors should give themselves suitable roles and relationships. Then, using music from the period and/or place in which the production is set, they can improvise a social dance. This extended improvisation should have four stages.

1. *Preamble*: In male and female groups, a discussion about their hopes and fears of the forthcoming dance [*10 mins*].

2. *Invitation to Dance* [*5 mins*].

3. *The Dance*: Dancing in the style of the period and/or place in which the play is set [*10 mins*].

4. *The Outcome*: Whatever happens after the dance; i.e. another dance, an intimate conversation with the dance partner, returning to the gender groups to talk about the experience, etc. [*10 mins*].

⚡ *Status Improvisations* (*page 54*)

With the whole cast working together as a group, but not necessarily using their characters from the play, the actors should give themselves roles and relationships that reflect the roles and relationships of their characters in the play. Then they can do an improvisation which explores the status differences of the characters in the play [*15 mins*].

🔥 *Drama Triangle* (*page 56*)

Ask three actors to cast themselves as a family. Then say that one is to be a persecutor, another is a victim and the third is a rescuer. Ask them to improvise a family scene [*10 mins*].

Then get them to keep the characters and swap the roles around and improvise another family scene [*10 mins*].

Thirdly, they should still keep their characters, but each person should take on the role they haven't yet explored and they should do a third family improvisation [*10 mins*].

⚡ *Specific Background Improvisations* (*page 59*)

Depending on the requirements of the play, the actors can improvise scenes to help them understand any specific details of the play which are not within the range of their own experience.

Chapter 4 – Preparing a Character (*page 71*)

The following improvised exercises are like a series of sketches to help the actors build a clearer picture of their character so they can then start more in-depth improvisations. For these exercises, the whole cast should work at the same time, but each actor should work on their own.

◣ *Centres* (*page 74*)
The actors should experiment with different physical centres for their character until they find one that seems to be the most suitable [*15 mins*].

◣ *Energy States* (*page 76*)
The actors should experiment with different energy states for their character, ranging from 'Catatonic' to 'Rigid', until they find one that seems to be the most suitable [*15 mins*].

◣ *Animals* (*page 82*)
The actors should experiment with becoming different animals to help them find the 'soul' or inner life of their character until they find one that seems to be the most suitable. Then they should 'humanise' the animal [*15 mins*].

◣ *Bringing the Character to Life* (*page 84*)
Using the discoveries from the last three exercises, the actors can combine the 'animal' version of their character with the 'centre' and the 'energy state' versions [*15 mins*].

◣ *Exploring the Details* (*page 87*)
Using the results of all these exercises, the actors, as their characters, can explore various simple activities; i.e. sitting in a chair, entering a room, running for a bus, etc. [*10 mins*].

Continuing as their characters, the actors can then experiment with how their characters relate to other human beings by having simple conversations with each other. For this exercise they should imagine that their character doesn't know any of the other characters in the room [*10 mins*].

Chapter 5 – Developing a Character (*page 89*)

Having created a rough sketch of a character, each actor can start to develop their character through a series of solo exercises and improvisations.

▪ *Getting Dressed* (*page 93*)

Using the research information about the clothing of the period and/or place in which the production is set, each actor should decide what their character would wear and then improvise putting their clothes on in the morning, item by item [*10 mins*].

▪ *Shopping for Clothes* (*page 95*)

Working in pairs, one actor should be his or her character and the other should be a shop assistant (or appropriate equivalent). They should improvise a scene where the character buys some new clothes. This would include a discussion about the effect that each item of clothing would have on the character's appearance [*10–15 mins*].

▪ *Letters Home* (*page 96*)

As their character, each actor should write a letter to a member of their family or a close friend about how they are feeling and what is happening in their life. This should take place at a point in time before the action of the play [*20 mins*].

This solo improvisation can be used later in rehearsals to examine how a character might feel at any point during the action of the play.

▪ *Helping Each Other* (*page 98*)

The whole cast should each 'become' one of the characters in the play while the actor playing that character watches their work. They should explore the physicality and the vocal mannerisms of the character [*10 mins per character*].

▪ *Like-minded Friends* (*page 99*)

Each character in the play can improvise a scene with three or four other actors who take on similar characters; i.e. Juliet with a group of fourteen-year-old girls, Isabella (in *Measure for Measure*) with a group of novitiates [*15 mins*].

⚡ *Going Out in Character* (*page 101*)

Each actor should wear the sort of clothing their character would wear if they were alive at the present time, and then they should 'become' their character and go outside and interact with people in the real world; i.e. going shopping, going to a café, asking someone the way, etc. [*2 hrs*].

Chapter 6 – Relationships (*page 104*)

The relationship that each character has with other characters in the play can be explored through improvisation.

⚡ *Family Relationships* (*page 107*)

If any of the characters in a play are members of the same family then a series of improvisations can explore the changing moods and experiences of family life [*10–15 mins per improvisation*].

⚡ *Previous Good Times* (*page 110*)

If any characters in the play have a difficult, troubled or disastrous relationship, then they can explore how the relationship went wrong by improvising a time when the relationship was more positive. This could be a series of improvisations to explore the development of the difficult relationship [*10–15 mins per improvisation*].

⚡ *Friendships* (*page 112*)

If any of the characters in the play are close to each other (family, friends, work colleagues, neighbours, etc.), then they can improvise a time when they first realised that they had something in common. This can develop into a series of improvisations to explore the way the friendship has evolved [*10–15 mins per improvisation*].

⚡ *Evolving Relationships* (*page 114*)

If a group of characters in the play have known each other for a long time and have met on a regular basis, then a series of improvisations can explore the way their relationships have evolved [*10–15 mins per improvisation*].

Chapter 7 – Centre of Attention (*page 123*)

The following improvisation explores aspects of a character that might not have occurred to the actor playing the part. It also gives the actor the opportunity to 'be' their character for an extended period of time.

⚡ *Centre of Attention Improvisation* (*page 126*)

Each character can become the centre of attention in a group of people who want to find out all about them.

In groups of four or five actors, one character from the play is chosen to be the centre of attention. A decision should be made about what the scenario should be.

The actor who is going to be the centre of attention should leave the room and 'become' their character.

The other actors should each decide what their character will be, what their area of interest is and what the relationships are amongst the group. Everyone should know what all the others have decided.

If it is suitable, someone should invite the centre of attention character to come into the room for their interview or meeting. If, however, the action takes place in a less formal environment, such as a bar, then the character should just 'arrive' when the rest of the group is ready.

The improvisation should take place with everyone staying truthful to the situation and their characters [*20 mins*].

After the improvisation there should be a discussion about what has been discovered. The director can take this opportunity to suggest any adjustments to the character that they feel will help.

Chapter 8 – Sense Memory (*page 133*)

Various emotional incidents that a character might have undergone but which are not within the experience of the actor playing the part can be explored through improvisation.

⚡ *Sharing a Sense Memory* (*page 137*)

If two or more characters in a play have shared a particularly strong emotional experience in the past, then the actors should try to recreate the events that caused them to have that emotional experience [*20 mins*].

⚡ *Physical Sense Memory* (*page 138*)

If a character has a particular physicality that is different from that of the actor playing the part, then whatever causes or caused that physicality can be explored through exercises and improvisations.

⚡ *Emotional Memory* (*page 140*)

Any emotion or event that is outside the experience of the actor can be explored through exercises and improvisations.

Chapter 9 – Creating a History (*page 148*)

Using any information that can be gleaned from the text, and in discussion with the actors, a series of improvisations can be used to explore previous events that would have influenced a particular scene in the play.

After each improvisation there should be a discussion about what has happened and that discussion can inform the substance of the next improvisation.

Chapter 10 – Preparing to Rehearse (*page 155*)

When the cast is ready to start rehearsing the text of the play they can be eased into the work by the following exercises and improvisations.

Learning the Lines (*page 156*)

Before any explorative work on a scene, the actors should be thoroughly familiar with their lines. The line-learning can be done during the period of rehearsal that is devoted to character and relationship improvisations.

Starting Work on a Scene (*page 158*)

Ask the actors to wander around the room, running the lines of a scene without worrying about where they should be onstage. As they do this they should listen to the other actors and then respond to them with their own lines. They should also try to communicate the meaning or intention of their lines to each other as they speak.

Playing the Intention, not the Emotion (*page 159*)

In a highly charged emotional scene, the actors should be reminded to communicate the meaning of the words that their character says, and not let that meaning be overwhelmed by emotion.

⚡ Pre-scene Action (*page 161*)

The actors should improvise five or ten minutes of action that could have happened before the scene starts [*5–10 mins*].

⚡ Entrances into a Scene (*page 162*)

If a character enters during the action of a scene, the actor, in discussion with the director, should decide what they think their character has been doing up until the moment they arrive. If they have been with people who are not going to be in the scene – like a taxi driver, a servant who has answered the door, or a person in another part of the house – then other members of the cast can take on the necessary roles.

When the improvisation starts, the actors who are in the scene already should stand by. When the new arrival seems to be about to enter, the director should signal for the other actors to start the final few lines of text before their entrance. Once the entrance has happened, the scene should continue for a few minutes using the text as written [*10 mins*].

This should be followed by a discussion in order to evaluate the improvisation and make the appropriate adjustments before doing the improvisation again.

Chapter 11 – Developing a Scene (*page 166*)

Once the actors are using the text of the play, there are various improvisations that can give them a greater understanding of a scene.

⚡ *Improvising a Scene in Your Own Words* (*page 169*)

If the play is in heightened language, or the language structure and/or vocabulary of the play is different from that of the actors, then they can improvise the scene using their own words.

⚡ *Improvising the Subtext* (*page 173*)

There are several ways to isolate and emphasise the subtext:

Vocalising the Subtext: The actors should play the scene using the text, but after each phrase, they should speak the subtext quietly.

Playing the Subtext: The actors should improvise the scene speaking the subtext instead of the written text to create dialogue.

Physicalising the Subtext: The actors should play the scene using the written text, but as they say each phrase they should make a physical gesture to express the subtext.

Thinking the Subtext: The actors should play the scene using the written text. As they do it they should make sure they think about the subtext as they say each phrase but they should try not to let it show.

⚡ *Improvising the Dynamics* (*page 178*)

If there is a moment in the play when something unexpected happens to any of the characters, then an improvisation can be set up secretly by the director to create a similar unexpected event.

⚡ *Improvising a Crowd Scene* (*page 179*)

Each member of the crowd (non-scripted parts) should create a character and various relationships with other members of the crowd. They should then be allowed to improvise a crowd scene in the appropriate location but without the main characters present.

The scripted scene should then be performed with the main characters, but each member of the crowd should feel free to react in any way they feel is appropriate to the character they have created.

⚡ *Improvising the Objectives* (*page 182*)

In discussion with the director, the actors should analyse a scene, section by section, and make a note of the changing emotions and objectives so that a series of improvisations can be set up to explore each of them in isolation. This will enable the actors to develop a clear understanding of their characters' desires and at the same time allow them to fully experience any emotion that their characters might be trying to conceal.

⚡ *Improvising the Essence of a Scene* (*page 184*)

If the characters in a scene are behaving in a stereotypical manner, then the scene can be played by taking the essence of that stereotypical version and playing to the hilt. For example, if two characters are being childish, let them play the scene as if they were children. If one character seems to be interrogating another, let them play the scene as if it really was an interrogation.

⚡ *Improvising Using the Text* (*page 187*)

Using the text, the actors can isolate and emphasise the varying dynamics of a scene.

⚡ *Blending Improvised and Scripted Dialogue* (*page 188*)

If the scene involves a number of characters in a fairly active situation, then improvised dialogue can be used alongside the scripted dialogue.

Problem-solving (*page 189*)

When a scene doesn't seem to be working, then an improvisation can be created to shed new light on it and help the actors solve their problems.

THE IMPROVISATION BOOK

How to Conduct Successful Improvisation Sessions

From the author of *Improvisation in Rehearsal*, *The Improvisation Book* takes the reader step by step, session by session through a graded series of improvisation exercises starting with the very first class – full of inhibited first-timers – then adding a new element at each session until the once bashful students have a full vocabulary of improvisational techniques. John Abbott has devised a unique set of Improvisation Cards. Picked at random by the actor, these cards determine what Character is to be played – Do-Gooder, Egoist, Hypochondriac, etc. – and in what Scenario – a Job Interview, a Blind Date, etc. The almost endless combinations provided by these cards ensure that the leader need never run dry! The complete set of 96 cards is included in the book – to be cut out or photocopied as preferred.

'A veritable treasure trove... Abbott's book is of real value in the training of actors; I'm enthused and excited about putting it into practice' *ReviewsGate.com*

'Distils a lifetime of experience and is set out logically and practically so that would-be actors can build skills from the very simple to the remarkably complex' *British Theatre Guide*

978 1 85459 961 2   £10.99 IN UK ONLY

Available from all good bookshops and from
www.nickhernbooks.co.uk